Aquatic Turtles

Complete Herp Care

David T. Kirkpatrick

Aquatic Turtles

Project Team
Editor: Thomas Mazorlig
Copy Editor: Mary Grangeia
Cover Design: Cándida Moreira Tómassini, Mary Ann Kahn
Design Team: Mary Ann Kahn, Patti Escabi

T.F.H. Publications
President/CEO: Glen S. Axelrod
Executive Vice President: Mark E. Johnson
Publisher: Christopher T. Reggio
Production Manager: Kathy Bontz

T.F.H. Publications, Inc.
One TFH Plaza
Third and Union Avenues
Neptune City, NJ 07753

Printed and bound in China,

07 08 09 10   3 5 7 9 8 6 4 2
ISBN 978-0-79382885-2

Library of Congress Cataloging-in-Publication Data
Kirkpatrick, David T. (David Thomas), 1965-
Aquatic turtles : a complete guide to sliders, cooters, maps, and more / David T. Kirkpatrick.
p. cm.
Includes bibliographical references and index.
ISBN 0-7938-2885-6 (alk. paper)
1. Turtles as pets. 2. Aquatic animals. I. Title.
SF459.T8K56 2006
639.3'92--dc22
2005036185

The Leader In Responsible Animal Care For Over 50 Years!™
www.tfhpublications.com

Table of Contents

It always helps when your family enjoys your hobbies as much as you do, so a very large thank-you goes out to my wife Catherine and daughter Alia for their participation in our turtle-keeping adventures. Thanks also go to Ed Kowalski, who was responsible for convincing me to write my very first turtle article over 18 years ago. I'd also like to thank those who were members of the New England Herpetological Society during our time

Acknowledgments

in Boston, including Roberta Dell'Anno, Marie Girard, Jayme Gordon, Mike Labbe, Joe Martinez, Dawn McCall, Tom Monahan, Rick Roth, Allison Schacht, Kurt Schatzl, Jerry Smith, and Tom Spadaro. Finally, this book is dedicated to Rick and Mary Stafford, for all of their help and advice over the years, and for their many years of dedication to herpetoculture.

We all miss you, Rick and Mary.

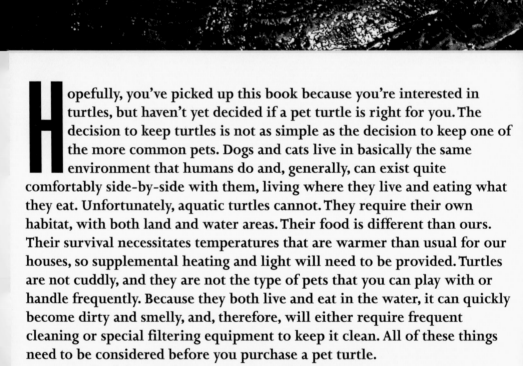

Hopefully, you've picked up this book because you're interested in turtles, but haven't yet decided if a pet turtle is right for you. The decision to keep turtles is not as simple as the decision to keep one of the more common pets. Dogs and cats live in basically the same environment that humans do and, generally, can exist quite comfortably side-by-side with them, living where they live and eating what they eat. Unfortunately, aquatic turtles cannot. They require their own habitat, with both land and water areas. Their food is different than ours. Their survival necessitates temperatures that are warmer than usual for our houses, so supplemental heating and light will need to be provided. Turtles are not cuddly, and they are not the type of pets that you can play with or handle frequently. Because they both live and eat in the water, it can quickly become dirty and smelly, and, therefore, will either require frequent cleaning or special filtering equipment to keep it clean. All of these things need to be considered before you purchase a pet turtle.

Given all of the conditions I mentioned in the previous paragraph, why would anyone even consider keeping turtles? If you are willing to put in the

Read Me First

time, care, and effort that turtle keeping requires, they can make fascinating pets. While you can't play with them, they are intelligent animals that exhibit a large range of interesting behaviors. They quickly grow to recognize the people that they live with and the daily and weekly patterns that surround them. If treated correctly, turtles can live for decades—depending on the type of turtle and its age when acquired, you may have this pet for 30 to 60 years or longer. I have some turtles in our house that we've kept for over 20 years, and they were at least that old when they first joined our household. It is quite possible that my young daughter may be passing some of them on to her children-to-be, long after my wife and I are gone.

The keys to successful turtle keeping are simple: knowledge, desire, and effort. The more information you have about turtles and how to keep them correctly, the better they will do. The more desire you have to keep them successfully and provide them with the best care you can, the better they will do. Finally, the more effort you exert to care for them appropriately, the better they will do. A turtle keeper who combines all of those elements will find that turtles are endlessly fascinating animals to have around.

Chapter 1

An Overview of Turtles

When most people think of pets, a turtle isn't the first animal that pops into their minds. However, with proper care and attention to their needs, turtles can be kept as pets with great success. Unfortunately, many people don't know how to go about keeping them, and their efforts lead to disaster, especially for the poor turtle. As is true with many of the animals that fall outside of the dog/cat/hamster range of pets, careful preparation, knowledge of the animal's needs, and a willingness to take the extra steps necessary to provide a proper home are the essential ingredients for proper turtle care. This book will provide the basic information necessary to provide a suitable environment for the long-term health and prosperity of a turtle. Depending on the type of turtle, a keeper is quite likely to be outlived by the animal in his or her care. Unlike most pets, turtles have a potential life span that can be longer than that of most humans, leading to the possibility that a pet turtle will be passed down from generation to generation.

What Is a Turtle?

The word *turtle* comes to us from the French word *tortue*, which is also the root of the word *tortoise*. Turtle is the generic name for all reptiles that possess shells. In the United States, *turtle* is used colloquially to refer to the semi-aquatic species that inhabit lakes, ponds, and rivers or their margins, while *tortoise* is reserved for those species that live exclusively on land, only entering water for a drink or a quick wallow. Land tortoises are distinguished by the shape of their legs, which often remind people of those of elephants. Finally, some species of turtle are called terrapins. The name *terrapin* was originally used for turtles that were harvested for food, such as the diamondback terrapin (*Malaclemys terrapin*) found on the eastern seaboard of the United States. This term has fallen out of favor and is now rarely used in the 05.

Regardless of what name they are called, turtles are instantly recognizable. Their shells give them away every time, even for those species like the softshell turtle, whose shell isn't quite what people have in mind when they think of a turtle. Their shell, in addition to being their most recognizable feature, is the main reason behind their success as a group—turtles have outlasted the dinosaurs and are found on every continent, except Antarctica, as well as in most of the world's warm-water oceans.

The Evolution of Turtles

Turtles are an ancient group of animals. They are one of the main branches of the class Reptilia, along with lizards, snakes, crocodilians, amphisbaenids, and the very ancient tuatara. Turtles are distinct from these other reptiles by a number of different characteristics, including their shell and the structure of their skull, which has a solid cranium lacking the openings present in other types of reptiles.

Reptiles, in general, arose from an older group, the amphibians. Amphibians were the first group of vertebrate animals to become adapted to long-term life on land. However, amphibians still require a water source for reproduction, as their eggs are not protected from dehydration. Reptiles became distinct because they gained adaptations that allowed them to virtually sever their ties with water. They have a scaly skin that does not require frequent wetting, and, in fact, its toughness prevents the loss of water from the body of the animal. Reptiles also have internal rather than external fertilization, so they do not require an aquatic environment for mating. Also, reptile eggs have a tough outer layer that prevents the eggs from dehydrating during development of the embryo, unlike the eggs of

The Turtle in Legend and Myth

Worldwide, turtles can be found in the myths and legends of numerous cultures. They are often portrayed as stoic, solid, dependable creatures that can be relied upon for aid and comfort. For example, many North American Indian tribes have tales that mention the turtle or afford them elevated status as representative animal spirits. Native people of South America and the Pacific Islands have many folktales that involve land, freshwater, or marine turtles, depending on the location of the particular group.

Some of these tales have spread across the globe and have been incorporated in one way or another into cultural folklore. An example is the familiar tale, *The Tortoise and the Hare*. In a footrace between the two animals, the speedy hare is easily distracted from the task at hand—winning the race—while the slow tortoise perseveres and eventually wins the race, much to the surprise of the hare. Usually, stories of this kind use the perceived positive aspects of the turtle to impart a moral or reinforce a desired virtue or action.

Turtles play an important role in some religions, especially during the genesis of the world or the cosmos. A number of creation myths involve a turtle supporting the world on its shell or serving as the beginning of the land area amidst a vast ocean. A number of Buddhist temples in Asia have resident populations of turtles that are considered to be holy in nature. Visitors to the temples feed them in hopes that their holiness will be passed on to those aiding them. In addition, turtles are often depicted as very long-lived creatures, if not immortal ones. This quality unfortunately has led to the practice of consuming turtles, or turtle parts, in order to "capture" their essence and thereby increase the health or vitality of the person eating the animal. In some parts of Asia, the trade in turtles for food has severely impacted turtle populations.

amphibians, which have no protective covering beyond the gelatinous mass in which they are laid. In addition, each reptile egg contains its own nutrients and water supply, allowing reptiles to lay their eggs on dry land. These adaptations gave reptiles the ability to colonize land areas that do not have permanent water sources, and they quickly spread to cover all of the continents of the ancient world.

A female oblong turtle (*Chelodina oblonga*) demonstrating her side-necked nature.

The oldest fossils recognizable as turtles to have been identified so far date back over 200 million years. These fossil turtles originated in the Triassic period. While they display many differences from modern turtles, they are not great enough that a casual observer would not recognize them as turtles. These ancestral turtles were probably aquatic in nature.

The Two Divisions

The two modern groups of turtles arose significantly later. The first group, Cryptodira, is represented in fossil records during the late Jurassic period, while the second group, Pleurodira, appeared during the Cretaceous period. Cryptodira are the more numerous forms of turtle. They originally appeared in freshwater and land habitats, but some forms later colonized the oceans. The pleurodiran turtles are confined to freshwater habitats and currently are found only in the Southern hemisphere—in South America, Africa, Madagascar, and the New Zealand-Australia region of the south Pacific.

The characteristic that distinguishes these two main divisions of turtle is the manner in which their necks bend as they retract their heads into their shells (or try to, as there are turtles whose shell and head structures no longer permit them to retract their heads). Cryptodira, which arose first, fold their necks in a vertical dimension. Pleurodira fold their necks horizontally, in a side-to-side manner, which gives this group their common name, side-neck turtles. While the pleurodiran turtles arose approximately 40 to50 million years after the cryptodiran turtles, herpetologists consider them to have more primitive characteristics than the cryptodiran turtles.

The Turtle Groups

Modern turtles are still divided into the two main groups that arose alongside the dinosaurs: Cryptodira (hidden necked) and Pleurodira (side-necked).

Two different families of turtle are recognized within the Pleurodira. Pelomedusidae consists of five genera (plural of *genus*, the level above species) of turtle: *Pelomedusa* and *Pelusios* from Africa, *Erymnochelys* from Madagascar, and *Podocnemis* and *Peltocephalus* from South America. Chelidae consists of nine genera: *Chelodina, Elseya, Emydura, Pseudoemydura, Rheodytes,* and *Phrynops* from Australia, and *Hydromedusa, Chelus,* and *Platemys* from South America.

Ten different families of cryptodiran turtle have been described by herpetologists. Dermatemydidae, Carettochelyidae, Platysternidae, and Dermachelyidae are all represented by only a single species each. Dermatemydidae is represented by *Dermatemys mawaii*, the Central American river turtle, Carettochelyidae by *Carettochelys insculpta*, the pig-nosed turtle, Platysternidae by *Platysternon megacephalum*, the big-headed turtle, and Dermachelyidae by *Dermochelys coriacea*, the

Herpetology and Herps

Herpetology **is the study of reptiles and amphibians. For this reason, both reptiles and amphibians are often called** *herps***. Hobbyists who keep them as pets are often call** *herpers, herp hobbyists,* **and** *herpetoculturists***. The last term is usually applied to those hobbyists and professional keepers who breed their herps.**

Emydidae is the turtle family that contains the greatest number of species, represented here by the western painted turtle.

Two Kinds of Neck

The two main groups of turtle are Cryptodira (the hidden-necked turtles) and Pleurodira (the side-necked turtles). The terms refer to the two different methods the turtles use to retract their head into their shell.

leatherback sea turtle. Chelydridae has only two representatives, but they are both very well-known—the common snapping turtle (*Chelydra serpentina*) and the alligator snapping turtle (*Macroclemys temminckii*). Cheloniidae has four living species; all are found in the oceans. These are *Chelonia* (the green and flatback sea turtles), *Lepidochelys* (the Ridley sea turtles), *Caretta* (the loggerhead) and *Eretmochelys* (the hawksbill).

The majority of the cryptodiran turtles fall into the four remaining families: the Kinosternidae, which consists of about two dozen species of mud and musk turtles; the Trionychidae, comprising about two dozen species of softshell turtles; the Testudinidae, with about fifty species of tortoises, and the semi-aquatic pond turtles of the family Emydidae, which is the most numerous with approximately ninety species.

The species of turtle that are most likely to be maintained in captivity by turtle keepers fall into these four families, and this book will cover the care and maintenance of all of them (except tortoises, which require drastically different enclosures and maintenance methods). The third section of the book gives specific descriptions of a number of different types of aquatic turtles that are in these families.

The Biology of Turtles

Turtles are unique in the world, with features that are found in no other animals. They share many characteristics with the other reptiles, such as being cold-blooded, possessing a relatively tough skin, and laying leathery or hard-shelled eggs that result from internal fertilization during mating. However, the most obvious feature of the turtle is also its most unique—its shell.

The Shell

A turtle's shell is composed of two or three parts, depending on the species of turtle. The upper portion of the shell is called the carapace, while the bottom portion is known as the plastron. In most turtle species, there is a distinct region found on each side between the front and back legs that joins the carapace and plastron. Fittingly, this junction is called the bridge. Some turtles, however, lack bridges—the plastron and carapace merge together directly. The North American box turtle (*Terrapene carolina*) is one such turtle.

The origin of the turtle's shell is quite interesting. It probably developed as a result of the fusion of bones from the turtle's rib cage and spinal column with the free-floating bony plates (osteoderms) embedded in the proto-turtle's skin. The bones of the ribs and vertebrae widened and flattened in the process and can still be seen underlying the bones of the carapace in the skeletons of many species. The shell can take on many different shapes and dimensions, depending on the species of turtle: very domed in land tortoises, flattened and disc-shaped in pond turtles, or elongated and ridged as in the leatherback sea turtle and in snapping turtles. In some species of turtle, the bones of the shell have undergone a reduction in size and thickness. This occurs in a number of species that inhabit the water, probably to reduce the turtle's weight. The most dramatic example of this reduction is seen in the pancake tortoise, whose carapacial and plastral bones are paper thin, with large openings between them.

The outer covering on the shell of most turtles is not a layer of bone, but a hard material more closely related to fingernails and claws. This layer is divided into small plates, known as scutes. The divisions between scutes occur in the same approximate location as the divisions between bones, but the match is not exact. As a turtle grows, new layers of scute material are deposited under the old from a layer of cells between the bones and the scutes. Some turtles retain each scute layer, giving each one a pyramidal appearance and causing others to look as if each scute has a growth ring, like those seen in tree trunks. In those species that have a winter resting period, a new scute layer forms in the spring and summer, so the "growth rings" actually are annual. However, many turtles shed layers of scute material and, in those that don't, the top layers often wear away over time, making the counting of rings an inaccurate way to measure a turtle's age. Finally, some turtle species have done away with the scutes entirely, and the underlying skin has toughened, becoming leathery. These turtles, the softshell turtles of the family Trionychidae and the marine leatherback, have sacrificed the added protection of the scute layer for a reduction in weight that increases their maneuverability and speed.

Cold-Blooded Terms

Animals that are ectothermic (cold-blooded) regulate their body temperature by interacting with their environment by engaging in behaviors like basking. Animals that are endothermic (warm-blooded) regulate their body temperature internally through metabolic processes that generate heat.

Vertebral Scutes

Carapace

Nuchal Scute

Scutes

Marginal Scutes

Bridge

Plastron

Turtle Terms

bridge: **connection between the carapace and the plastron.**

carapace: **the top part of the shell.**

marginal scute: **the sections of the carapace forming its outer border.**

nuchal scute: **the marginal scute directly over the head and neck of the turtle; absent in some species.**

plastron: **the bottom part of the shell.**

scute: **the individual sections of the shell.**

vertebral scute: **the scutes of the upper shell lying direction over the vertebral column.**

In some species of turtle, the plastron has a movable hinge running from side to side. This hinge allows the turtle to move portions of the plastron up or down, aiding the turtle in sealing up the shell against predators. The North American box turtles (*Terrapene* spp.) are well-known for their hinge, which occurs about a third of the way down the plastron, just behind the front legs. Mud turtles (*Kinosternon* species) have hinged plastrons also, but in these turtles there are two hinges, giving the turtle the ability to raise both the front and back edges of the plastron. One group of tortoises, the hinge-backed tortoises of the genus *Kinixys*, have a rudimentary hinge that runs across the back quarter of the carapace, allowing the tortoise to pull the carapace down slightly to protect its back legs and tail.

The Body

Everybody is aware that the limbs, head, and tail of a turtle all project outward from the interior of its shell, but few people stop to consider what that means. The front legs of a turtle are attached to its shoulder girdle, and the rear legs are attached to its pelvis, just as they are in other animals and humans. However, the placement of these bone structures is quite different—they are located within the turtle's rib cage! During the evolution of the turtle's basic body plan, the turtle's shoulders and hips migrated inside the shell, which is a modified rib cage. This placement creates unique difficulties for the turtle, especially regarding its ability to breathe. Most animals rely upon the movement of their diaphragm and rib cage to assist in the inhalation and exhalation of air.

Musk turtles—a common musk turtle, or stinkpot, is shown here—get their name from the pungent oil they secrete when being handled.

However, the rigidity of the turtle's rib cage and the location of its limbs prevent it from using this method of breathing. Instead, the turtle relies on small movements of its front or back limbs, coupled with movements of muscles in its throat, for assistance in the act of breathing in and out. If you watch a turtle at rest, such as when it is basking on a log with all of its legs stretched out,

you will notice that it occasionally pulls some of its legs into its shell slightly, and puffs out its throat. It is doing these movements in order to breathe.

All turtles breathe air, even the giant marine turtles. However, turtles that live in the water have a number of adaptations that allow them to remain underwater for extremely long periods of time. They have relatively slow metabolisms, and so a breath of air can be made to last a long time, especially if the turtle is resting on the bottom, waiting for food to wander by. In fact, during winter hibernation, some turtles remain dormant on the bottom of ponds or streams for months at a time. Some turtles also "mouth-breathe" when they are underwater— they fill up and then empty their mouths repeatedly. The mouths and upper throats of these turtles are heavily lined with blood vessels that are close to the surface of the skin. It is thought that this allows oxygen trapped in the water to be passed into the blood supply, thereby increasing the length of time that the turtle can remain underwater. Some aquatic turtles also can draw water into their cloaca and then expel it, presumably for the same reason. The cloaca is the single opening on the turtle's tail that houses its reproductive organs and through which it excretes waste material. It is also call the vent.

Special Traits

Finally, some turtle species have special traits that aid in their survival. A number of groups, most notably the mud and musk turtles, possess glands near the bridges of their shell that secrete an oily liquid that has a very strong odor; this musk gives the turtle its common name. The alligator snapping turtle has a small pink tentacle in its mouth that it can wriggle. Resting quietly underwater with its mouth gaping wide open and its tentacle wriggling like a worm, the turtle will lure unwitting fish into its mouth, where instead of biting the "worm," they become the turtle's dinner instead. The South American matamata employs a unique form of camouflage: it has all of its limbs, head, and tail covered with shreds of skin, breaking up the turtle's outlines and making it look like a pile of leaves. The snake-necked turtles of South America and Australia have necks that are incredibly long— in some instances significantly longer than the body of the turtle. This kind of neck allows the turtle to breathe without surfacing and to capture prey that is not close to the turtle itself.

Why the Decline?

The main reasons behind the worldwide decline in turtle populations are habitat loss and exploitation by man, including use of turtles for food, folk medicines, pets, and souvenirs.

The Conservation Status of Turtles

Unfortunately, the long-term outlook for most turtle populations is not good. The very qualities that human cultures have admired about them, such as their slow but deliberate nature, have made it difficult for the turtle to survive in the face of

The bog turtle is a protected species in the US. Habitat loss is the biggest threat to the species' continued survival.

increasing pressures from human populations. The turtle's shell, which has kept it safe from predators for millions of years, is no match for an automobile or the quick and deadly hands and tools of men. Similarly, their relative slowness makes it difficult for turtles to migrate away when humans begin to alter their environment through the construction of roads and buildings, or the draining, diversion, or modification of lakes and rivers.

Many scientific researchers and environmental organizations have been monitoring the status of turtle species across the globe. The first reason for loss of turtle populations is the ongoing modification of their natural habitat. The last two centuries have seen a huge increase in the rate of conversion of wild areas to agricultural use. The destruction of the native ecologies present in an area usually lead to the loss of any turtle populations, as the animals are no longer able to find the proper food or successfully breed in the new situation. Logging of forests dramatically alters the balance of the region, also potentially leading to a loss of appropriate habitat for turtles.

One of the most significant modifications with regard to local turtle populations is changes to the waterways—drainage of wetlands, diversion of rivers, conversion of estuaries to human activity, and beachfront modifications, all of which negatively impact turtles. While it is true that some human alterations create novel turtle habitats (rice paddies that support Asian pond turtle populations, for example), these increases are insignificant in comparison to the losses.

Four-inch Law

One federal law that concerns turtles is the so-called "Four-inch Law," which prohibits the sale of turtles that are less than four inches long. This law was passed in reaction to a number of publicized cases of salmonella poisoning that were linked to the improper handling of pet turtles. Enforcement of the law can be rather arbitrary; in some areas of the country, the law is rarely enforced, while in others it usually is.

The second main reason for turtle declines is direct exploitation by humans. In general, turtles are harvested by humans for four main reasons: food, medicinal use, the pet trade, and decorations or souvenirs. The relative percentage of each type of harvesting varies from region to region, but in general the largest losses occur because of food and medicinal harvesting. This trend is especially prevalent in Asia, where native populations are declining at alarming rates.

In the past, only specific turtle species were harvested for food; the diamondback terrapin in the United States is a good example. However, in some parts of the world, demand for turtle meat has increased to such a degree that any species of turtle is acceptable. In addition, certain species of turtle have gained a reputation of having medicinal qualities—the flesh of an Asian box turtle, *Cuora trifasciata*, is rumored to be able to treat cancer, for example, even though no studies support this idea. Turtles from species with medical connections can command enormous sums on the open market, often hundreds of dollars or more per animal. These demands have led to a dramatic increase in international shipments of turtles to these areas of the world, and a dramatic drop in turtle populations in the areas exporting turtles to meet the demand. While the majority of the turtle trade involves countries in Asia, there have been increases in shipments of North American turtles such as red-eared sliders to China and other Asian countries.

Trade in turtles and tortoises is regulated at both the international level and on a country-by-country basis. The chief international treaty that influences the trade in turtles is the Convention on International Trade in Endangered Species of Wild Fauna and Flora (CITES). CITES keeps active lists and records of endangered and threatened species, and those animals and plants on the CITES lists are prohibited from trade without the proper permits in countries that have signed the CITES agreement. Also, a majority of governments base their national regulations on animal trade on the CITES regulations. If these international and national regulations were followed, the trade in endangered turtle species would be drastically reduced or prevented. Unfortunately, enforcement of the laws does not occur to the degree necessary to aid native turtle populations. Given the global extent of the problem, conservation groups are beginning to consider placing all of the world's turtle species on the threatened or endangered lists as a first attempt to rein in the potentially disastrous loss of native populations.

Although hatchling turtles, like these painted turtles, are adorable, it is illegal to sell turtles that are less than four inches long in the US.

The United States supports the CITES agreement, and many of the laws concerning trafficking in animals are modeled on the CITES regulations at the national level. Finally, most states have enacted their own set of laws that govern local populations of turtles, especially if a threatened or endangered species is present in the state. These laws usually regulate the capture and possession of native turtles. Even some local communities have regulations concerning exotic pets that may include provisions about turtles. While a thorough coverage of the large number of state and federal laws governing turtles is well beyond the scope of this book, in general, the state laws fall under the fisheries and wildlife section of the government; copies can be obtained from them. Local herpetological societies are also very good sources of information on the local and state laws that affect the keeping of reptiles, including turtles.

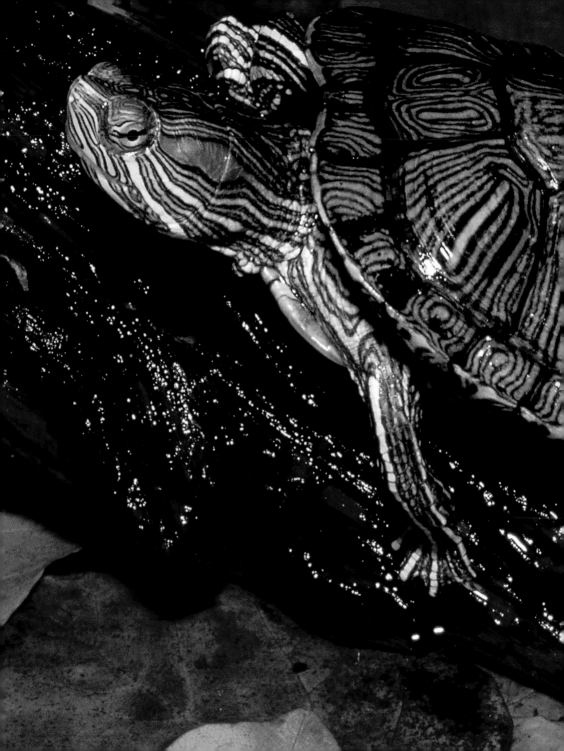

Chapter 2

Keeping Turtles

Turtles, while familiar to everyone, remain fascinating creatures to many people. Everyone can picture a turtle basking in the sunlight, stretched out on a log in the middle of a pond. Pictures like this often cause people to consider keeping a turtle as a pet. However, to be successful with turtles, a number of factors must be taken into account. Proper husbandry is a necessity, of course. This section covers all of the factors that a turtle keeper must bear in mind when caring for an aquatic turtle.

Initial Considerations

When you first consider the idea of keeping a turtle, you should ask yourself a number of questions. First and foremost: Why do I want one? If you are interested in the turtle itself, that's a good reason. However, if you are interested because it is an exotic animal to keep as a pet, you might want to consider other exotic animals. Aquatic turtles are significantly harder to keep than many other animals because of their specialized environmental needs. If you are interested in the turtle only because of its exotic nature, you will have a lot of time in which to grow bored of it, as chelonians (another term for turtle) can live a very long time.

Once you've decided upon acquiring a turtle, other questions that you should consider are: What kind should I get? Where will I obtain it? Where should I keep it? How will I take care of it? The answers to all of these questions will be covered in this book, but the first and most important question can only be answered by you, preferably before you purchase a turtle!

You must be prepared before acquiring a turtle; they live a long time and have specific needs. A striped mud turtle is shown.

Once you have decided upon keeping a turtle, you will need to do a bit of research before acquiring it. Unlike many of the most common pets, detailed preparations are required before purchase to ensure that the turtle will thrive in its new environment. You will need to determine three things: what type of turtle you want to get, what type of enclosure you will keep it in, and where you will obtain the turtle. These decisions will be influenced by each other—for example, if you decide to keep a very large turtle, some types of enclosures will not be suitable for it. Similarly, if you decide on an exotic turtle, then you will be quite limited in your choices of places that might be able to sell you a turtle of that kind. Finally, if you want to display your turtle for all to see, the need for an awe-inspiring enclosure will likely dictate both the type of display and the types of turtle that will be appropriate.

Beginning turtle keepers should start with an abundant local species of turtle. Turtles that are native to the area will not need to adjust to

Captive-bred Is Better

If at all possible, buy a captive-bred turtle. Captive-bred turtles are usually more healthy than wild-caught ones—especially if the wild-caught turtle in question was imported from some distant land. Captive-bred turtles are normally free of the parasites, diseases, and wounds that are commonly found in wild-caught individuals. Additionally, captive-bred turtles are already adapted to life in captivity, so there is far less chance one will fail to acclimate to the habitat you provide it.

different climates or seasons, nor will they have endured the stresses of transport. This is why it is often easier to keep and breed local turtle species than exotic ones. If at all possible, start with captive-bred turtles. Choose an animal that is alert and active. If you tug lightly on a leg, there should be firm resistance. Inspect the shell and skin for cuts, abrasions, or discolored spots that might indicate sores or infections. Finally, have any turtle you purchase (captive bred or wild caught) examined by a veterinarian skilled with reptiles.

The setup for your turtle should be completed and functioning before you bring it home. This allows time to monitor for problems in filters, heaters or in the arrangement of the tank. It is a lot harder to patch a leaking land area when the tank is full of turtles! Having the enclosure up and running also places less stress on the newly arrived pet, allowing it to adjust more quickly to its new environment.

Deciding on Which Turtle to Keep

Choosing an appropriate turtle is very important. Final size of the turtle is often a major factor in deciding which species to keep. A number of the more commonly available turtles can grow to a large size. Sliders may reach a foot or longer in size, depending on the specific species, while snapping turtles can get even larger. Do not buy a turtle just because it looks interesting; find out what type it is, read up on it, and decide if you can provide it with a good home. This chapter will give a quick overview of some of the most common turtles kept in captivity. Chapter 6 discusses each turtle in greater detail. Finally, a number of good books have been published that present comprehensive information on individual turtle species; books that you might want to consult are listed in the References.

Some Common Turtles

In the United States, by far the most commonly available aquatic turtles are the red-eared slider and its close relatives. Sliders, cooters, painted turtles, and map turtles all resemble each other superficially and require similar care. Their shells are disc-shaped and relatively flat. Sliders

The red-eared slider has been the most commonly kept turtle for several decades.

and cooters are hardy turtles and usually do well in captivity. However, they grow quite large, with some types approaching two feet (61 cm), although most common species only grow to about 12 inches (30.5 cm) in length. Painted turtles are smaller and somewhat less hardy, while map turtles require the most attention to thrive.

Table 1: Commonly Kept Turtles

Scientific Name	Common Name	Location	Max. Size
US Species:			
Trachemys scripta elegans	Red-eared Slider	Southeastern US	M: 7.9 in (20 cm), F: 11 in (28 cm)
Chrysemys picta	Painted Turtle	US	10 in (25.4 cm)
Pseudemys floridana	Florida Cooter	Southeast coast, US	15.8 in (40.3 cm)
Graptemys geographica	Common Map Turtle	Central US	M: 6.3 in (16 cm), F: 10.6 in (27 cm)
Sternotherus odoratus	Stinkpot or Musk Turtle	Eastern US	5.4 in (13.7 cm)
Kinosternon subrubrum	Eastern Mud Turtle	Southeastern US	4.9 in (12.5 cm)
Kinosternon baurii	Striped Mud Turtle	Southeast coast, US	5 in (12.7 cm)
Kinosternon flavescens	Yellow Mud Turtle	South-Central US	7.2 in (18.2 cm)
Chelydra serpentina	Common Snapper	East of the Rockies	19.4 in (49.4 cm)
Trionyx spiniferus	Spiny Softshell Turtle	Central US	M: 8.7 in (22 cm), F: 21.3 in (54 cm)
Exotic Species:			
Chinemys reevesii	Reeves Turtle	China, Korea, Japan	9.1 in (23 cm)
Mauremys mutica	Asian Yellow Pond Turtle	Southern China	7.7 in (19.5 cm)
Cyclemys dentata	Asian Leaf Turtle	From India to China	9.5 in (24 cm)
Pelusios subniger	African Mud Turtle	Southeastern Africa	7.9 in (20 cm)
Chelodina species	Snake-necked Turtle	Australia	to 15.7 in (40 cm)
Hydromedusa species		Brazil, Argentina	to 11.8 in (30 cm)
Platysternon megacephalum	Big-Headed Turtle	From Burma to China	7.2 in (18.2 cm)

For those keepers interested in smaller turtles, mud and musk turtles are fascinating creatures, and most are less than half the size of the sliders and painted turtles. Unlike the saucer-shaped slider, mud and musk turtles have taller, steep-sided shells that are longer than they are wide. While their brownish color scheme is drab compared to the colorful slider, what they lack in appearance they make up for in personality. Mud and musk turtles have lived for 50 years in captivity; with proper care, they are quite hardy.

A wide variety of exotic turtles are intermittently available, such as leaf turtles, African mud turtles, and snake-necked turtles. Juvenile snapping turtles and softshell turtles are also sold, but their large adult size and aggressive behavior make them unsuitable for all but the most dedicated turtle keepers.

Overview of Commonly Available US Species

Red-Eared Sliders By far the most easily recognized turtle in the United States is the red-eared slider (*Trachemys scripta elegans*). This turtle was the original dime-store turtle, until the Federal Government banned the sale of hatchlings and juveniles less than four inches in length in 1975 due to salmonella poisoning concerns. Red-eared sliders over four inches long are still sold as juveniles in pet stores nationwide, and thousands of hatchlings are shipped outside the United States each year. Although many people remember sliders as little turtles the size of a quarter, few realize that if fed and housed adequately, they can grow to be almost a foot in length (30.5 cm). Their carapaces are disc-shaped and green, with thin yellow stripes or blotches. The underlying coloration of their skin is green also, but with yellow stripes or dots on the legs and face. As their name implies, there is a red spot or wide stripe behind each eye. Closely related turtles that have different patterns and lack the red "ear" are sometimes found in pet stores. Some of these species can reach two feet in length! Adult male red-ears have longer tails than females, and they have distinctive sword-like front claws. Adults will require a large aquarium, especially the females, which grow noticeably larger than the males. A 75- to 100-gallon (about 284-379 l) aquarium would be suitable for an adult pair of red-ears, for example.

A basking site is a necessity for red-eared sliders. They will climb onto it and sun themselves under the lights for hours at a time, with legs outstretched to absorb the warmth. In their natural habitat along the Mississippi River and its tributaries, they can often be found basking in just this manner. Sliders are hearty and omnivorous feeders if kept warm enough (water temperature in the upper 70s (24°-26°C), basking area in the upper 80s (29°-31°C)). A varied diet of vegetables, insects, meat, fish, and earthworms is essential. With proper care, a captive life span of over 20 years is quite possible—one turtle was still alive at a reported age of 41 years.

Not So Little Turtles

You might be surprised to know that the familiar red-eared slider can grow to almost a foot in length if it receives the proper care. If you keep one, you must remember that eventually it will need a large aquarium. Plan ahead.

A number of other turtles can be kept in a manner similar to red-eared sliders. These include Florida cooters (*Pseudemys floridana*), painted turtles (*Chrysemys picta*), and map turtles such as the common map turtle (*Graptemys geographica*). Florida cooters resemble red-eared sliders, but have less decoration and a higher domed carapace. They grow somewhat larger—up to 16 inches in length. They are more herbivorous than sliders. In the wild, they congregate in large groups to bask; sometimes two dozen or more may be piled on a single log.

Painted Turtles Painted turtles, on the other hand, are smaller than red-eared sliders. They are very attractive turtles that have a black shell edged with red markings and dark skin with thin yellow and red stripes. Painted turtles do not grow quite as large as the red-eared slider. Somewhat shy in disposition, they startle easily. They are not quite as hardy as red-eared sliders and are prone to infections if a high level of cleanliness is not maintained. Interestingly, they are the only turtle that ranges across the entire continent, with differing subspecies found in the eastern, midland, southern, and western portions of the country.

Map Turtles Map turtles, although perhaps the most striking of the "slider" type of aquatic turtles, are the most difficult to keep successfully. They are brilliantly patterned chelonians, with fine striping on their shells and skin. Different species can be distinguished by the form these patterns take. Very wary and nervous turtles, they live in clean rivers and streams in the central and southern portions of the United States. In captivity, they require pristine water conditions. Their enclosure should be placed in an area that gets little traffic, as they stress easily. The sexes are quite dimorphic, with females growing to just under twice the size of males. Map turtles should be kept only by someone with experience in keeping turtles and a willingness to devote a lot of effort and care to them.

Although map turtles (Texas map shown) are interesting and colorful animals, they have strict keeping requirements.

Mud and Musk Turtles Almost diametrically opposed to the sliders group in appearance, size, and habit are the mud and musk turtles (*Kinosternon* and *Sternotherus* species). Where the slider is large, brilliantly colored, and highly visible, the mud turtle is small, drab, and secretive. I have heard the musk turtle described as a "scrawny mouse hiding in a turtle shell"—the description, although not elegant, certainly fits. However, they are interesting turtles with a lot of fascinating behaviors. They often adapt well to captivity. One musk turtle, acquired as an adult, lived at the Philadelphia Zoo for almost 55 years! Although not as attractive as the slider, painted, or map turtles, their small size and hardiness make the mud and musk turtles attractive choices for the novice turtle keeper.

While all four species of *Sternotherus* are found in the United States, only five of the 16 species of *Kinosternon* are located there; the rest occur in Central and South America. The common musk turtle (*Sternotherus odoratus*), the eastern mud turtle (*Kinosternon subrubrum*), the striped mud turtle (*K. baurii*) and the yellow mud turtle (*K. flavescens*) enter the pet trade most frequently. All are smaller turtles: the largest, *K. flavescens*, can reach seven inches, while *K. baurii* and *K. subrubrum* don't exceed five inches and are often much smaller. Their shells are more rectangular than those of the sliders and painted turtles, with almost vertical sides. The different species can be distinguished by shell characteristics or markings and by patterns of striping on the skin. The striped mud turtle has three distinct lines running the length of its carapace, while the yellow mud turtle has a very light tan or yellow shell coloration. Mud turtles have hinged bottom shells similar in function to the hinges on box turtles; the musk turtles lack hinges. The plastron is also reduced in size in musk turtles.

Loggerhead musk turtles and most of the other members of their family are small and hardy turtles that make good pets.

Due to their small size relative to the slider, mud and musk turtles do not require as large an enclosure. A pair of turtles can be maintained in a 30-gallon (114 l) aquarium quite nicely. As might be expected by their secretive nature, these turtles are not fond of basking, so the basking area does not need to be very large. However, one should still be provided. Although they are called mud turtles, a muddy bottom is not essential for their maintenance and probably should be avoided due to the problems it causes in terms of water cleanliness. Mud and musk turtles prefer to have an underwater retreat; one can be provided with rocks, wood, or plastic. Make sure that the retreat cannot collapse on the turtle, trapping it underwater and eventually drowning it.

The mud and musk turtles are generally omnivores and will accept different types of plant and animal food in captivity. Mud and musk turtles often find their food by poking along the bottom of streams, rivers, or ponds. As most of the prepared foods float, it may take wild-caught turtles some time to recognize turtle pellets as edible.

Snappers and Softshells Two other types of turtles occasionally show up in pet stores: snappers and softshells. However, both turtles are not suitable for the beginning turtle keeper. Snapping turtles (*Chelydra serpentina*) are large turtles, with a carapace half-way between mud turtles and sliders in shape. Their heads and heavily scaled limbs are very powerfully built. The plastron is reduced in size to an even greater extent than in musk turtles. Snappers grow to be quite large; turtles of up to almost 20 inches (0.5 m) have been reported. Snappers live up to their name, especially when out of the water. Due to their large size and temperament, they are not appropriate for novice turtle keepers. Juveniles may look interesting, but they will quickly grow to an unmanageable size.

Softshell turtles (*Trionyx* species) are bizarre looking turtles in that they resemble flying saucers as much as anything else. They are highly streamlined and adapted for moving rapidly through water. As the name indicates, the carapace and plastron of softshells are leathery and flexible. Their limbs end in feet that are heavily webbed and flipper-like. They have a very long neck and a head that has a very long nose with the nostrils at the very tip. Softshells are fond of burying themselves in soft sandy bottoms, and their neck and nose arrangement allow

Think Twice

Snapping turtles and softshells are large and aggressive turtles. They often reach sizes of 18 inches (45.7 cm) or more. Both types of turtle can inflict a severe bite. If you think you want either of these leviathans, consider carefully before you buy one.

them to breathe without surfacing. Some species of softshell grow larger than snappers. The largest of these are generally female; males are quite a bit smaller than the females.

Softshell turtles can be difficult to keep in captivity. Their sheer size requires a very large turtle tank. They can be prone to infections from cuts or abrasions on their shell. In general, they are aggressive and are capable of delivering nasty bites. Because equally interesting and much more easily kept turtles are available, snappers and softshells are best observed in their natural environment.

Overview of Commonly Available Exotic Species

Most of the turtles that you might encounter in your average pet store are native to the United States. If at all possible, a beginning turtle keeper should start with a local turtle species.

Common snapping turtles grow too large for the average keeper to easily care for.

However, if you have some experience with turtles or can find captive-bred specimens, you might want to consider buying an exotic turtle. Decide which turtle you wish to work with, and find out all you can about it. This will enhance your chances of success.

Exotic turtles (unless captive hatched) have undergone a stressful process: capture, multiple shippings, and exhibition in a pet store. Once purchased and an appropriate environment for the turtle determined and provided, exotics must still adjust to altered seasons and the presence of people. All of this stress, combined with probable poor handling, can lead to low survival rates in imported chelonians. A veterinary examination of newly acquired turtles is very important.

Reeves' Turtles One of the most commonly seen exotic aquatic turtles is the Reeves' turtle (*Chinemys reevesii*). It is a small, hardy turtle with a lot of personality and has been successfully captive bred. It usually does not grow as large as a painted turtle and is more rectangular in shape. Three keels, or ridges, run the length of the carapace, which is often colored some shade of brown. The Reeves' turtle's skin is green with yellow stripes, but some individuals are very melanistic with a skin and shell that is very dark brown or black.

Like the snappers, softshells are too large and aggressive for most keepers. A Florida softshell is pictured.

Imported from southeast Asia, including China, Taiwan and Korea, these turtles do well if given the same type of care as sliders and painted turtles. As they do not grow as large, a Reeves' turtle habitat does not have to be as large as that of a slider, although success in breeding often requires a very large tank. In their native environment (streams, lakes, or ponds), Reeves' turtles are omnivores. In captivity, they will eat many different types of vegetables, insects, earthworms, and fish, as well as prepared turtle foods.

Asian Yellow Pond Turtles and Leaf Turtles

Two turtles, the Asian yellow pond turtle (*Mauremys mutica*) and the Asian leaf turtle (*Cyclemys dentata*), resemble the Reeves turtle in overall size and shape. However, they are not as colorful, generally being solid yellow or brown. They are both omnivores, and a varied diet is essential for keeping them in good health. As they are somewhat more terrestrial than painted turtles or sliders, a larger basking or land area can be provided. Other than that, the care for these turtles is the same as for a Reeves' turtle or a slider. Both the leaf and pond turtle adapt well to captivity if given the appropriate environment and care.

Summary Sleep

Some turtles enter a summer dormancy period, called aestivation, usually triggered by high temperatures and droughts and dry spells.

African Mud Turtles Exotic turtles often enter the United States in waves. As one source for turtles dries up, importers turn to other sources and other species. The hardy African mud turtle (*Pelusios subniger* and related species) has been a large part of a recent burst of arrivals from Africa. Although called mud turtles, these turtles more closely resemble painted turtles in both general appearance and habit. Usually, the carapace of an African mud turtle is some shade of brown, while their skin is yellow, ivory, or gray, occasionally with a delicate vermiculated pattern of darker color. They derive their name from their habit of digging into muddy areas to escape the hottest portion of the African summer. This ability to aestivate may contribute to their hardiness—imported African mud turtles seem to survive the rigors of capture and transport better than other species. Enclosures suitable for sliders will serve African muds quite well. They are avid baskers, but if a land area is provided, they will occasionally bury themselves for a few days, as they do in their native environment.

Other Exotic Species A few other species are seen in ordinary pet stores, but to find more exotic turtles you often need to turn to reptile dealers. Most of these exotics, including the ones I will mention next, are not suitable for beginning turtle keepers. However, in the past I have seen some specimens of snake-necked turtles and big-headed turtles in pet stores; as it is possible that they might once again enter the pet trade, I will describe them so that you can identify them if necessary. These imported turtles are so unique that you won't be able to forget them once you've seen one!

Snake-necked turtles (of the species *Chelodina* and *Hydromedusa*) are aptly named. Their necks are very long, often almost as long as their shell. *Chelodina* is Australian in origin, while *Hydromedusa* is found in South America. They are both mainly carnivorous, using their long necks to seize unsuspecting prey. Big-headed turtles (*Platysternon megacephalum*) are moderately sized turtles, with a long armored tail. Their most striking feature is their huge wedge-shaped head, which is too large to retract into their shell. These turtles have developed a layer of plates on their head for protection. In some respects, they resemble snapping turtles but are much more agile. In their native China, Vietnam, and Thailand, big-headed turtles are found in cold, rocky, mountain streams. They are adept at climbing and have been reported to climb trees. Big-heads are carnivorous and nocturnal, sleeping in the gravel at the bottom of streams during the day and emerging at night to chase their prey. They are poor swimmers and should be kept in a relatively shallow aquarium with a land area, although they will not bask.

Obtaining a Turtle

How and where you obtain your turtle will depend on the purpose for which the turtle has been acquired (as a pet or for breeding, or both), and how many turtles you are interested in purchasing at the same time. Obviously, if one of your main goals is to breed a particular species of turtle, you will need at least two turtles, or probably more, in order to have a hope of success at breeding.

The first decision will be whether to get a wild-caught turtle or a captive-born animal. If the turtle is to be a pet, try to locate a breeder of turtles, as captive-born animals have many advantages. Most notably, captive-born turtles are often much healthier than wild-caught animals and have been acclimated to life in captivity and the presence of people. The breeder that you purchase the turtle from has already worked out exactly how to keep that particular type of turtle in captivity. Usually, he or she will be quite happy to give you advice on keeping the animal that you acquire healthy. Finally, you can be sure that your purchase is not hurting any wild populations of turtle.

Another possibility is to adopt a turtle. Many herpetological societies and animal rescue programs take in unwanted turtles, rehabilitate them if necessary, and then look for a new home for them. Contact your local herpetological society or animal rescue society and inquire about adoption programs in your area.

If you cannot locate captive-born turtles, purchase a turtle from the local area. If you can't find a local species, it is a good idea to stick to North

The African mud turtles (*Pelusios castaneus* shown here) tend to fare better than many other imported species. .

American species. Much more is known concerning the natural history of North American turtles than of the more exotic turtles of South America, Africa, or Asia. Knowing the natural history of the animal makes it easier to design an appropriate enclosure and provide an adequate diet. Finally, know the local laws—many areas now regulate the removal of turtles from their natural environment, especially for those species of turtle whose populations are threatened or endangered. If you take a turtle from the wild, you may find yourself in serious trouble with the local wildlife officials.

Wild-caught turtles, whether native or imported, have been removed from their natural environment, which could be a disastrous loss for that population. These turtles are often stressed by their capture and transport, and therefore potentially unhealthy. In addition, they usually carry parasites that they picked up in the wild. However, for some species of turtle, a wild-caught individual is the only option, as they have not yet become established in captivity enough to have developed a substantial pool of captive-bred animals to purchase. Thus, you may be forced to purchase a wild-caught animal, especially if your goal is to breed a relatively uncommon species.

For breeding purposes, try to acquire turtles from the same area to lessen the chances of accidentally mixing up unknown subspecies. If the turtles are imported, get as much data as possible from the importer. Specific collection sites, habitats at the collection site, and similar data can be invaluable in setting up an appropriate captive environment.

Captive-bred turtles are usually healthier than wild-caught ones, especially species normally imported like these matamatas.

If at all possible, obtain your turtle locally, either through a pet store, a breeder, a reptile show, or a herpetological society. If you purchase the turtle directly, you will have the opportunity to observe it and, hopefully, compare it to other turtles. This first-hand observation will assure you that you are purchasing a healthy turtle of the species that you are most interested in. If, however, you cannot locate a local source, or the type of turtle you wish to keep, there are a number of companies that specialize in obtaining and selling reptiles, including turtles. Such companies can readily be located online. If you have contacted a local herpetological society, its members will be able to provide you with information on reptile dealers and steer you away from those that are not reputable. You may also be able to find individual turtle breeders online, which may be your best option for obtaining a particular type of turtle. Finally, there are a number of reptile and amphibian shows and exhibits held across the country that can be an excellent source of captive-born turtles.

Beware!

In the list below are signs that a turtle is unhealthy. Avoid turtles that display any of these characteristics:

- **Crust around or discharge from nostrils**
- **Eyes sunken, closed, or crusted shut**
- **Feces are bloody, runny, or full of worms**
- **Feels light or hollow when picked up**
- **Inactive and/or not alert**
- **Sores or wounds on the shell**

Choosing a Healthy Turtle

If possible, check the health of the turtle before purchase. Examine it for injuries, overall appearance, and sex. The turtle should be appropriately heavy for its size—if it feels too light, it probably is not healthy. The turtle's eyes should be clear and responsive. Its mouth should be clean; thick deposits of film or paste on the tongue or back of the throat are signs of an infection. Finally, the turtle should be active, pushing on your hands to get away, or pulling in its legs if they are lightly tugged. After acquisition, examine all animals, whether captive born, locally collected, or imported, for parasites (both internal and external), and quarantine the turtles appropriately before housing them with other animals. If you see any signs of illness or parasites, a visit to the local veterinarian is highly recommended, and it is good idea even if the turtle seems completely healthy.

Chapter 3

Turtle Care and Feeding

Thirty years ago, the federal government passed a law banning the sale of turtles with a carapace length of less than four inches. Although designed to prevent people from contracting salmonella poisoning, the ban probably saved untold thousands of baby red-eared slider turtles from an untimely death. The state-of-the-art turtle container at that time consisted of a foot-wide plastic bowl with a small island in the center on which stood a brown and green plastic palm tree. A healthy, well-fed red-eared slider hatchling would have outgrown it within two months. However, at that time the food sold for turtles consisted of dried ants and ant larvae. If kept at room temperature (as they usually were) and fed only dried ants, not even the very hardy red-eared slider usually survives.

Behavioral Thermoregulation

Turtles maintain an appropriate body temperature, or thermoregulate, through interactions with their local environment. For example, a turtle that is basking is increasing its body temperature through exposure to the sun and will cool off by periodically entering the water. This type of temperature control is called behavioral thermoregulation.

Thankfully, turtle care has progressed in the last three decades. Many different types of aquatic turtles can be raised, maintained, and bred when provided with the appropriate environment. This chapter discusses those requirements and gives a few tips for successful turtle housing.

Basic Requirements

There are many different types of enclosures, both indoor and outdoor, that are suitable for keeping turtles. However, all of them share a few basic characteristics—they provide adequate space, adequate light levels, and an appropriate amount of warmth for the turtles they house.

Size and Location of Turtle Tanks

The first major decision that a prospective turtle keeper must make, even before deciding upon the type of turtle to obtain, is where it will be kept. If you live in a location that has temperate weather for a large part of the year, you should consider maintaining your turtle outside. While there are risks and difficulties inherent in outdoor maintenance, exposure to full sunlight and natural conditions provide enormous benefits to the turtle, and you have the best chance of long-term success.

The majority of turtle owners keep their turtles indoors. Before deciding on a type of turtle to keep, you will need to decide how much room you can devote to its enclosure and where to locate it. For example, placing a turtle tank in a high-traffic area such as a kitchen or living room may lead to problems if you choose to keep a species that has a nervous disposition, such as a map turtle. Often it is better to locate the turtle tank in a spot that is away from the main areas of activity in the house.

As a rule of thumb, bigger is always better when it comes to indoor turtle tanks. For the turtles that I have kept, I provide water areas that are 4 to 5 times longer than the turtle, 3 to 4 times wider, and at least 1.5 times deeper than the longest dimension of the turtle. So, if you are considering keeping a painted turtle, which can reach 8 to 10 inches (20.3 to 25.4 cm) in length, a reasonable tank size would be 36 to 48 (91.4 to 121.9 cm) inches

Provide your turtle with a water area that is at least 1.5 times as deep as the turtle is long. A yellow-blotched map turtle is pictured.

long, 24 to 36 inches (60.9 to 91.4 cm) wide, and at least 12 inches (30.5 cm) deep. A water area of this size would give a painted turtle adequate swimming room and would also be deep enough to prevent injury or accidental drowning. If the water is too shallow, a turtle can injure its shell against the hard tank bottom when diving into the water. It can also be a drowning hazard—if the turtle accidentally flips over on its back in shallow water, it may not have enough water depth to flip back over and may drown if not rescued in time.

Naturally, if more than one turtle is being kept in a single enclosure, more area will need to be provided; I usually increase the dimensions by about 25 percent for each additional turtle. Juvenile turtles can be kept in smaller quarters, but they will grow and eventually require a larger tank. In the long run, it is usually cheaper to buy or construct a turtle enclosure that will accommodate an adult turtle, even if you are beginning with a juvenile or hatchling.

The amount of space that a prospective turtle keeper can devote to the turtle tank often determines the type of turtle that can be kept successfully. For this reason, smaller turtles such as mud and musk turtles are often more appropriate for novice turtle keepers—they do not require very much space and general care and maintenance of the enclosure is also

No Sunlight

If you are housing your turtle in a glass aquarium, take care not to put the aquarium in full, direct sunlight. If the turtle cannot get out of the sun, you may end up with a baked dead turtle.

significantly less arduous. Large tanks, beyond just their overall size, are quite heavy because of the large amount of water they hold. In addition, all of that water must be kept clean and changed periodically. Keep this in mind when deciding on a spot for the turtle tank. It should be located near a sink and drain to facilitate this. Finally, take into consideration the items surrounding the turtle tank. Be sure that nothing irreplaceable will be damaged if water splashes from the tank or the tank begins to leak.

Lighting

If you opt to set up outdoor turtle tanks or tubs, the sun should provide plenty of natural light if you place them in appropriate locations. Turtles that are kept indoors will require a light source during the day, unless the tank is placed in a room that receives a large amount of natural light. If it is kept in a low light area, you should provide a supplemental light source for the turtles. Two basic types of

If you keep your turtle indoors, you must provide supplemental lighting to the enclosure. Note that this slider needs a deeper water area.

lighting are used by turtle keepers: incandescent bulbs and fluorescent bulbs. Both types have their advantages and disadvantages, and, in many cases, both are used for lighting the same turtle tank.

Incandescent light bulbs usually provide a higher level of light in a concentrated area, as well as providing a heat source. In many turtle setups, incandescent bulbs in an aluminum clip light or a similar sort of spotlight are used to direct a high level of light and supplemental heat to a particular spot in the tank. Often, these spotlights are used to light and heat an area that will encourage the turtles to bask. If you set up an incandescent lamp as a spotlight for basking, take care to check the temperature at the basking spot and regulate the light level and intensity to prevent the area from overheating.

Although providing your turtle with ultraviolet light is not required, it is recommended, especially for hatchlings like this red-eared slider.

Fluorescent lighting usually provides a more even light level, but lacks the ability to provide a concentrated spot of light. Banks of fluorescent tubes are often used over large turtle tanks to provide a high level of general light, simulating the light levels on a bright, sunny day. Keep in mind which species of turtle is being kept—high light levels might not be appropriate for turtles that are mainly active at dusk, dawn, or during the night, but should be provided for active daytime turtles such as sliders or painted turtles.

Ultraviolet Lighting A final item that should be considered is a full-spectrum fluorescent light bulb. A number of different manufacturers produce fluorescent bulbs that are marketed as "full-spectrum." Studies on these bulbs demonstrate that they usually don't duplicate the full range of natural sunlight, but a number of them produce significant amounts of ultraviolet B radiation (UVB), which is the wavelength of light that is required by turtles to stimulate

Remember to Change the Bulbs

UVB production by full-spectrum bulbs drops over time, so plan on replacing these bulbs yearly. A way to remember when to change them is to write the date you installed the bulb on a small sticker attached to some inconspicuous spot on the fixture.

production of vitamin D3. In turtles and most other animals, vitamin D3 is necessary for proper calcium utilization.

In my experience, hatchlings raised on a balanced diet with adequate calcium and vitamin supplements do not require full-spectrum lighting or additional UVB radiation. Therefore, it is unlikely that adult turtles, which have a lower overall requirement for calcium, absolutely require this type of lighting as long as they are receiving appropriate levels of calcium and vitamin D3 in their food. However, any added benefit in vitamin D3 production by the turtles that may result from the use of these bulbs shouldn't be discounted—indoor maintenance of aquatic turtles is not ideal, and anything that increases the similarity to their natural environment should be considered carefully. Similarly, a full-spectrum light does deliver a more natural type of light, and this may have a beneficial psychological effect on your turtles.

If you decide to provide full-spectrum lighting, keep in mind that the beneficial wavelengths of light are blocked by glass or plastic, so do not put these materials between the turtle and the light source. To be fully effective, the lights also need to be close to the turtles; 12 to 18 inches (30.5 to 45.7 cm) is desirable. Also, UVB production by these bulbs diminishes over time, even though the light level does not appear to change. Because of this, we routinely replace full-spectrum bulbs once a year.

Photoperiod Some species of turtle are nocturnal or crepuscular (active at dusk or dawn). Other species do not bask and so will not use basking lamps very often. However, if any plants are kept in the enclosure, they will benefit from full-spectrum lighting, and providing such lighting certainly won't hurt the turtle. Nocturnal or crepuscular turtles will still require a normal day/night cycle. Because of this, you should use lights with a cycle keyed to either the outside environment (especially if the turtle is kept in a room with windows) or to the day length in their native environment. For convenience, the light or lights over your turtle tank can be controlled using an ordinary timing device to turn them on in the morning and off in the evening.

Seasonal variation in the light levels should be taken into account. For rooms with a large amount of natural light, artificial lighting might be unnecessary during the summer months, but should be considered for the short winter days. Timers for lights should be adjusted periodically to reflect the changing length of the day. This lengthening and shortening of the photoperiod signals the passing of the seasons and can act as a stimulus for mating if you are keeping multiple turtles with the intention of breeding them. Keep in mind the type of turtle, its native locale, and the range in day length present in its natural environment when deciding on appropriate day lengths. This might be more important for wild-caught turtles than for captive-born turtles, as the captive-born individuals may have already been acclimated to the changes in day length that occur locally.

Heating

Most people maintain a room temperature range of $68°$-$72°$ F ($20°$-$22.2°$C) in their homes. Unfortunately, while this temperature range is quite comfortable for people, it is too cool for most turtles. Therefore, an indoor tank will require supplemental heat to keep the turtle happy and healthy. Commonly, supplemental heat is provided by overhead heat lamps, submersible water heaters, or undertank heating elements.

The most common heating method is to use a water heater. A fully submersible water heater helps keep the water at a reasonable temperature year-round, as many water turtles prefer water temperatures that are above ambient room temperature. However, the temperature of the water will depend on the type of turtle that you keep, and, therefore, you should investigate the natural environment of your species if you are not sure of its requirements.

Big Bend sliders and many other species of turtles warm themselves by basking in the sunlight.

Most underwater heaters attach to the side of an aquarium with suction cups. Heaters like this should only be used in glass turtle tanks. Tanks made of plastic may melt or deform due to the heat given off by the heater. If your turtle is very active, it may become necessary to wall off the heater to prevent the turtle from damaging or breaking

Incandescent UVB

There are now incandescent bulbs that supply ultraviolet B. These tend to be expensive, but they last a long time, so long that it is more economical in the long term to buy these instead of a fluorescent bulb that will need to be replaced every year or so. These bulbs do generate a lot of heat, so you must use a ceramic fixture and monitor the temperature closely. They are otherwise excellent products. You can find them on the Internet and at pet stores that have good reptile supply sections.

it. Some keepers place the heater in a ceramic or clay pipe, and then direct a current of water through it to move the heated water out into the tank. A submersible heater in a pipe can be used in plastic tubs, as the hot glass of the heater won't come into contact with the sides or bottom of the tub. Finally, an aquarium thermometer should be used to check the temperature of the water. Many heaters are not accurate and require monitoring to assure that the desired temperature is maintained.

Supplemental heat can also be provided by heating lamps suspended over the tank. Regular incandescent light bulbs housed in aluminum clip lamp reflectors are often used to direct a beam of light onto a specific area of the tank that serves as a basking area and also provides heat, warming the basking spot and allowing the turtle to regulate its body temperature.

Another innovation being used more frequently for heating turtle enclosures is a ceramic infrared-emitting bulb. This heater fits ceramic incandescent bulb sockets, but rather than emitting light, all of the energy is emitted as infrared radiation, which warms up whatever it falls upon. These ceramic bulbs can be used both day and night, while incandescent light bulbs are only useful during the day. Heat levels can be adjusted by increasing or decreasing the distance between the bulb and the surface that is being warmed. You should carefully check the temperatures under the ceramic bulb to make sure that the area doesn't get too warm over time. If you decide to use the ceramic infrared emitters, they should be used with a ceramic light socket, as the cheaper plastic sockets will fail rapidly from the higher levels of heat.

Heating elements that fit under a tank and warm from the bottom generally come in two forms: a thin plastic sheet with flat heating elements or a thicker plastic mat with embedded heating elements. The first kind is attached directly to the bottom of the tank. When plugged into an electrical outlet, the electrical current is converted into heat that is directly transferred to the tank. These undertank heating sheets work best with glass aquaria and may be hazardous when used with other types of turtle tanks. The second kind of undertank heater is often referred to as a "pig blanket" because it was originally designed for use on barn floors to provide supplemental heat to livestock. Not too surprisingly given their origin, they are very sturdily constructed from heavy-duty plastics. Most types of turtle tanks can be set down directly on a pig blanket heater. Some have a built in thermometer or gauge, but these are often inaccurate; each blanket should be monitored after it is put in place to confirm that it is maintaining the desired temperature in the turtle tank.

Often, combining a number of these approaches provides the best heating option for the turtle. For example, in plastic tubs that aren't suitable for submersible water heaters, an undertank pig blanket plus an overhead basking lamp provides general heat and a basking hot spot. For a glass aquarium, a basking lamp and submersible water heater make a good combination.

A simple setup for a musk turtle. A pig blanket (white rectangle in center) provides heat for the turtle.

Indoor Turtle Tanks

One of the most common ways to keep freshwater turtles in captivity is in a glass aquarium. However, very functional habitats can be constructed out of large plastic tubs, from utility sinks, or even metal cattle troughs, as long as the setup meets the few basic requirements discussed above. Tank decorations can range from minimal to elaborate, depending on the desires of the turtle keeper. For example, if you wish to observe the natural behaviors of the turtle or to have a true display piece, a setup that duplicates

Nighttime Heating

Infrared-emitting ceramic heat bulbs can be left on all night because they do not produce any light. They will not disturb the turtle's day-night cycle.

its native habitat as closely as possible might be appropriate. At the other extreme, a minimalist setup might be used for its ease of maintenance. This section will discuss the various types of turtle tanks and give a few tips on picking an appropriate one for you.

Glass Aquaria

Glass aquaria come in only a few different shapes and sizes, making the choice of an appropriate tank relatively easy. The aquarium must be large enough to give the turtle adequate swimming room in both length and depth, as discussed in the basic requirements section. A 20-gallon aquarium should be the minimum size, but bigger is always better. Only juvenile turtles should be kept in smaller aquaria, and they will outgrow them, so you might as well start with a bigger tank and save yourself money! So-called "long" or "breeder" tanks are usually better investments than "high" aquaria, as they provide a larger surface area for your animals. Again, the water level should be deeper than the turtle is wide, because if the water is shallow and the turtle manages to land upside-down in the water it may not be able to flip back over and will drown. Also, there should be no place underwater in the tank where the turtle could get wedged in such a way that it cannot get to the surface to breathe. So, for these reasons and for the happiness of the turtle, larger aquaria are definitely better.

Glass aquaria are probably the most commonly used enclosure for pet turtles. A red-eared slider is pictured.

Substrate and Furnishings

The aquarium does not need to have decorations, nor does it require sand or gravel on the bottom. These actually make it more difficult to clean and are not necessary for the turtle. However, while tanks with almost no decoration are easy to maintain, some keepers feel that they look too sterile and may stress the turtles because they are not being kept in a natural looking environment. These keepers tend to opt for a much more elaborate, naturalistic enclosure.

Depending on the species, the bottom substrate could consist of sand, gravel, or a layer of silt, or could be left bare. You can provide piles of rocks, wooden logs, or cork-bark floats. Broken clay pots often make suitable underwater caves.

Tank decorations will increase the maintenance required to keep the water clean, as they provide inaccessible areas where dirt can accumulate. They must also be arranged carefully; if a turtle becomes trapped underwater by poorly designed cage decorations, it can drown before its plight is noticed. Plants, both aquatic and terrestrial, may need to be replaced periodically if provided, as they may become sources of food for the turtles. Finally, many turtles are active foragers, and will dig up or otherwise disturb aquarium decorations or plants while hunting for food.

Wide, Not Tall

Wide, flat aquaria are better for turtles than tall, narrow ones of the same capacity, as they provide turtles with more swimming area.

Land Areas

One necessity in the aquarium is an area that is totally out of the water on which the turtle can haul out and dry off. Worn driftwood, cork bark floats, or smooth flat rocks work well, as they are not likely to rub or scratch a turtle's shell as it climbs out of the water. Position a spotlight over the rock or wood to simulate the sun, allowing the turtle to bask. Most turtles do very well with this type of setup: a large, deep, undecorated aquarium with a spotlight over a flat rock out of the water on which they can dry off and sun themselves.

A land area makes the aquarium look more attractive and is also quite functional. It is an absolute requirement if you intend to breed your turtles, as they will need an area in which to bury their eggs. With no access to a land area, a female turtle will retain her eggs as long as possible and then drop them into the water or on her basking area. Retaining eggs for too long can injure a turtle. For example, an egg might rupture while still inside the female, leading to a massive infection.

The size and depth of the land area is determined by the type of turtle you keep. Larger turtles will need a deeper area than smaller turtles to bury eggs. When laying eggs, female turtles dig a narrow, deep hole using their back legs, so the land area needs to be deeper than the turtle's fully extended back legs can reach. Also, some turtles are more terrestrial than others, and so benefit from a large land area.

Aquatic Plants

If you decide to add aquatic plants to your turtle setup, water hyacinth, water lettuce, water lilies, duckweed, and aquatic grasses are good choices. These plants are generally available at local pet stores. Some keepers will use ceramic or clay pots for rooted aquatic plants, as these can be submerged and will provide some protection to the plant from digging turtles. Floating plants such as duckweed work well, as there is no chance they will be uprooted by active turtles.

Land areas can be constructed in aquaria by walling off a section of the tank with silicone aquarium sealant and appropriately sized pieces of glass or plastic. For example, one end of the tank can be walled off with a vertical or diagonal piece of plastic. More intricate arrangements are also possible. As an example, three pieces of plastic can be glued into a U-shape in the middle of the aquarium to create a suspended island in the tank—two of the pieces are positioned vertically, and the last runs horizontally between them at their bottom edge. This is a very economical use of the space because it lets the turtles pass underneath, allowing them to move from one end of the tank to the other without going up onto the land area. Access to the land area can be provided by conveniently placed rocks, wooden cork floats, or ramps constructed of plastic. Depending on the setup, the land area can be made accessible from both sides, but animals can still pass underneath it. If the land island is placed at one end of the tank, an underwater cave is created. Many turtles, especially mud and musk turtles, take advantage of naturally occurring underwater shelters created by rocks or tree roots and will use the artificially created cave in a similar manner.

Inexpensive Enclosures

If your turtle enclosure is not meant to be a display item, or you wish to cut back on cost or maintenance, suitable turtle tanks can be made from commonly available items. Translucent plastic storage tubs or bins make very good turtle tanks, for example. These tubs can be purchased in a wide variety of sizes and shapes, allowing you to choose an appropriately-sized tub for the turtle that it will house. These tubs are significantly cheaper than an aquarium of similar size. In addition, they are much lighter, making it easier to carry and manipulate during setup and cleaning. They can be set up quickly, and make good emergency or temporary turtle tanks. If you have a couple of turtles and one becomes ill or injured, a plastic tub makes a very good isolation ward for the animal. Finally, they are

A piece of Plexiglas cemented to the tank walls sets the land area off in the author's mud turtle enclosure.

much less prone to cracking or breaking. This characteristic is important at cleaning time—it is much easier to clean a plastic tub with a hose or in a basement utility tub than it is to clean an aquarium of similar size because of the difference in weight and the need to avoid breaking the glass.

Plastic tubs do have a number of drawbacks, in addition to their obvious lack of aesthetics. They are not clear, so observing your turtle is much more difficult. Also, because they are made of plastic, submersible water heaters are not recommended for warming the turtle's water unless they are placed in a PVC, ceramic, or clay pipe, to prevent contact between the hot water heater and the side of the plastic tub. There is a chance that any plastic that contacts an unprotected heater could melt, leading to a disastrous flood.

Heating for plastic tubs is usually accomplished by placing them on a pig blanket or by hanging an incandescent bulb or ceramic infrared bulb overhead. It is harder to modify the tub by adding Plexiglas divisions or islands, as described above for glass aquaria. The sides of the tub are too flexible, and the aquarium sealant used to attach the dividers will break away when they bend. As a result, basking areas for plastic tubs usually need to be made from free-standing elements. A submerged brick topped by a smooth sloped rock, piece of driftwood, or plastic ramp works well in these situations.

Land Ho!

For most enclosures, the land area can be filled with a mixture of potting soil and sand. If the land area is going to be used for egg-laying by the turtles in the enclosure, the soil should not be allowed to become compacted, as it will make it difficult for the female to dig out a nest for her eggs. In any situation where eggs might be laid, the dirt in the land area should be kept moist and checked periodically to identify any eggs laid surreptitiously by the turtle.

Many other things can serve as turtle tanks, as long as they fit the basic criteria for semi-aquatic turtle enclosures: able to hold water, able to be heated, and not likely to be dangerous to the turtle. Large tanks that can hold a number of turtles can be constructed from cattle or horse watering troughs, for example. These are often made from metal or a hard plastic. As they are designed to be used around large farm animals, they are solidly designed and constructed. Their large size and weight make them difficult to move around, especially once they have been filled with water, so a good filtration system (described below) is usually used with these types of enclosures.

Basement utility sinks can be readily converted for use as a turtle tank. Utility sinks have a number of desirable characteristics: they are relatively cheap, they are made of strong plastic that is designed to hold water, they have their own legs that raise them up without need for a support stand, and they have a built-in drain at the bottom of the tank. With the addition of a stopcock and hose below the drain, the tank can be rapidly emptied into a floor drain, making cleaning a quick and relatively easy chore. A land area can be attached to the back or side of the sink if one is needed for egg laying by breeding turtles.

Finally, turtle tanks can be built from scratch using any number of different materials. Fiberglass can be used to form a water-tight tank area and combined with a plywood land area. Heavy-duty plastic sheets can be cut and joined, either with solvents or by melting, to create turtle tanks in any desired shape. Plastic pond forms can be obtained from garden supply centers and incorporated into an indoor turtle tank. Tank designs are limited only by your imagination and construction skill, but keep in mind the needs of the turtles that will be housed in the enclosure during the design stage to ensure that the final product will be a suitable home for them.

Outdoor Enclosures

Depending on your location and the climate, you may decide to keep your turtle

A soil substrate in the land area will allow you to grow some plants, making for a more interesting enclosure.

outdoors for all or part of the year. This approach has advantages and disadvantages, and you will need to carefully consider them all before you decide that an outdoor setup is appropriate for your situation.

The main advantage of outdoor maintenance is that it will, if done properly, provide the turtle with the most natural environment. Such an environment might be a very important consideration—for example, if you are planning on breeding your turtles, an outdoor enclosure may provide you with the best chance for success. The exposure to actual sunlight, proper day lengths, and the possibility of hunting and eating wild food items will benefit your turtle significantly. Outdoor setups allow for a very large water area relative to what is usually possible in a room or basement. The larger water area will act as a buffer, and the frequency of water changes will be reduced (but not eliminated!), especially if the water supply can be supplemented by natural rainfall and a water pump used to constantly circulate the water.

The main disadvantages of outdoor maintenance are the area that the enclosure will take up in your yard and the need for a secure enclosure to prevent predation. Any outdoor enclosure will need to be very secure in order to keep the turtles from escaping and to prevent predators from reaching them. They will need to be fully enclosed, with a secure roof, walls, and door system, and with a foundation that runs too deep to tunnel under. Enclosures that meet all of these requirements can be expensive to construct. As it will become a permanent feature of your yard, you will likely want it to be reasonably aesthetically pleasing.

Plastic tubs can be turned into simple and affordable turtle enclosures.

Finally, the location of the enclosure has to be carefully considered because the needs of the turtles have to take precedence, which means that it may need to be placed in a location you might not otherwise choose to put it. Also, keep in mind that many turtles may not be able to spend the winter months outside, especially in areas that experience extended cold spells. These turtles may require space indoors for those months, even if part of the winter is spent in hibernation. The need for this type of arrangement will vary depending on the climate in your area, of course.

Size

Once you have decided to construct an outdoor turtle enclosure, you will need to decide upon its overall size. The length and width of the setup will depend on the amount of ground that is available, the desired size of the water area, and the size and number of turtles that you will keep in the enclosure. The final height of the enclosure is only dependent on whether or not you want to be able to stand or walk in it. The turtles will not care if the sides are three feet high or seven feet high (0.9 to 2.1 m)—both heights will be equivalent in their ability to keep them in the enclosure. Some turtle keepers build tall enclosures that they can walk around in. Some even have space for a garden bench and table next to the water area so they can sit and watch their turtles whenever they want. Other keepers opt for a low enclosure in which the entire roof is hinged to serve as the door or doors. These two types of turtle pens are equivalent from the turtle's viewpoint, as long as they are properly sited, well-built, and secure.

Location

The first consideration in constructing an outdoor turtle pen is the location. An area should be chosen that experiences direct sun for a significant portion of the day. However, a section of the pen should always be shady, either because of nearby trees or bushes or because the pen has been built with shade-creating features. Constant full sun can lead to overheating, especially during the middle of the summer, which can be lethal to the turtles. Access to water may not be sufficient if the water itself heats up to a very high temperature; the turtles could still suffer heat stroke. Another consideration is the slope of the ground where the enclosure is constructed. The best spot is a gently sloping area, as this allows excess rainwater to drain away from the pen. If it is built in a depression or low spot, a severe rainstorm could flood the pen, potentially damaging the pen, ruining the landscaping, or even drowning the turtles.

An outdoor enclosure allows your turtle more space than most indoor enclosures can. African serrated mud turtles, *Pelusios sinuatus*, are pictured.

Construction of Outdoor Habitats

Once an appropriate location has been identified, a foundation for the walls should be constructed. In order to prevent the turtles from tunneling out of the pen, or other animals digging in, it should be dug at least a foot below the surface. The foundation itself can be made from a number of materials,

Something to Consider

as long as it is resistant to decay from contact with the damp ground. Brick, concrete, retaining wall stone, and the various plastic wood replacements all work well. The inside and outside trench bottoms can be lined with a layer of stones or a plastic mesh that is attached to the foundation, or both. This lining increases the safety of the turtles, as it further prevents successful tunneling. The stone layer may also help prevent decay, as it allows water to drain away from the foundation. Once the foundation and lining have been constructed, the trench can be filled in.

If you are building a low enclosure, the foundation walls can serve as the side walls also. However, if the enclosure will have high walls, these can be built separately and then attached to the foundation. Pressure-treated 2" x 4" (about 5 x 10 cm) lumber is often the material of choice. A pattern similar to that used in the construction of interior house walls can be implemented, but instead of covering the boards with wallboard, a wire mesh is attached with stainless steel staples (to prevent rusting). Plastic-coated mesh works well because it is resistant to rusting. Some keepers will attach a second layer of boards over the mesh to prevent any possibility of the mesh being pulled away from the inner boards by predators such as raccoons. All four walls and the ceiling can be constructed in this manner. One wall will require a door, but an opening can be framed in the correct wall, and a door can be made of the same materials as the walls. A heavy-duty bolt with a padlock should be used to secure the door and to prevent access by predators and inquisitive neighborhood children.

For low enclosures, the side walls can be solid, rather than mesh, as they will not block an appreciable amount of sunlight. The ceiling, which will also serve as the door,

Turtle Accessories

should be constructed of lumber and mesh as described above. It can be constructed as one piece, or divided into two pieces. If one piece, the whole ceiling should be hinged on one side, and locking bolts or clips attached to the other sides to secure it to the walls. If two pieces, either side can be hinged. A lock can be installed in the middle where the two pieces meet. This two-door system is usually easier to open and close, as each door weighs less and is not as awkward to move. However, they often sag in the middle where they meet, and reinforcing posts might be required under them at the midpoint to provide additional support for their weight.

Water Areas

Construction of the water area can be done either before or after the foundation and walls are constructed. A wide but shallow hole will need to be dug in the enclosure. The size, shape, and depth of the hole will be dependent on the layout of the water area and the type of pond (purchased or home-built) that is desired.

Many larger garden supply stores sell heavy-duty plastic pond inserts that come in various sizes and shapes. These inserts are suitable for use in a turtle enclosure, if a few considerations are kept in mind. First, the sides of these plastic ponds are often steep. This presents a problem to the turtles, as it makes it difficult for them to exit the water area. A slanting ramp of some kind must be provided to aid the turtles. Second, these ponds are relatively expensive for their size. If the enclosure will hold a large turtle or multiple turtles, the water area provided by one of these ponds may not be sufficient.

Basking species will benefit from exposure to natural sunlight in an outdoor enclosure.

Multiple ponds can be used, with a stream flowing between them. These are often constructed with allowances for pumping systems, which will keep the water flowing and clean.

Rather than relying on a pre-made plastic pond, a home-built pond can be constructed. Mark the desired extent of the water area on the ground, and then dig out a hole. At least one side of the hole should be gently sloping to provide an exit ramp for the turtles. Heavy-duty plastic pond or pool liner is then laid into the hole. Take care to avoid wrinkles and folds whenever possible, as these will trap dirt and debris and make it harder to keep the water area clean. Many keepers then put down a layer of smooth round stones or gravel. Larger rocks that project above the water can be used to provide basking areas. Smooth rocks with slanted sides that begin below the water line work best because they minimize the potential for damage to the turtle's shell from constant dragging over rough stone. Wooden logs or boards can also used. If the water area is large enough, these basking sites should be positioned in the middle; turtles are more comfortable if their perches are surrounded by water and, therefore, less accessible to predators.

A filter and water recirculation pump are very useful for outdoor turtle ponds. These can be purchased from garden centers or from websites. They should be positioned in the pond in a manner that will prevent the turtles from moving or damaging them. Also, a diffuser should be attached to the water intake pipe of the pump. Otherwise, it is possible for a turtle's shell to be sucked up against the end of the pipe, trapping the turtle underwater where it will drown if not rescued in time.

Landscaping

Landscaping Landscaping inside the enclosure is entirely at the discretion of the turtle keeper. An open area that is relatively sandy should be provided if there is the potential for egg laying. In high-walled enclosures, larger plants and bushes can be included. These can be placed in locations that will provide partial shade for the pond area during a part of the day. As mentioned, every enclosure should have a portion of the interior that is shaded throughout the day. The shaded area can change throughout the day, as long as at least one section is shaded. For very large enclosures, a seating area with benches, chairs, and even a table can be constructed. If the mesh lining the walls is small enough, the turtle enclosure can be a welcome bug-free retreat during summer evenings.

Choosing plants appropriate for an enclosure is complicated by the need to avoid plants that might be toxic to your turtles. Unfortunately, most of the information available on toxic plants is based on a plant's effect on mammals. Reptiles may react quite differently to these plants; box turtles have been seen to consume mushrooms that are known to be deadly to humans, for example. Many websites maintain lists of toxic plants, and these lists can serve as a starting point for plants to avoid, but keep in mind that plants that are not on the list may pose health risks to your turtles. Some plants that are usually considered to be relatively safe for turtles are ferns, spider plants, pothos, dracaena, day lilies, ficus trees, mulberry bushes, and hibiscus.

Maintaining Turtles in Captivity
Handling

Turtles are not the kind of pets that should be handled frequently. However, you will need to pick them up periodically in order to examine them or move them around. In general, most turtles are easy to handle, if care is taken. Be cautious when picking them up, as turtle shells can be quite slippery, especially if they have a layer of mud or algae on them. A fall onto a hard floor can severely injure a turtle. Newly captured or extremely stressed musk turtles will exude a yellowish compound from glands under the rim of their shells. This liquid has a rather pungent odor, thus the common name for the group (although mud turtles also possess the glands). Captive individuals usually lose this habit quickly. Even newly-hatched turtles are capable of producing musk and will do so readily if disturbed. Those species that grow to a large size are capable of delivering a strong bite and should be handled with care. In particular, softshell turtles and snapping turtles are known for their tendency to bite, in addition to a rather fierce temper that does not diminish with

Water lettuce—shown here with a young Florida softshell—is a safe aquatic plant that you can grow in your turtle enclosure.

length of time in captivity. For these reasons, handling of these two types of turtles should be kept to a minimum.

Turtles should be picked up by the shell, and not by the limbs, tail, or head. While you might be tempted to pick up a turtle by the tail in order to avoid a bite (especially a large and potentially dangerous one like a snapping turtle), doing so may injure it. The best way to pick up a small- or medium-sized turtle is to grab the shell from the rear, supporting the plastron with your fingers and palm, and pressing down on the carapace with your thumb. This grip puts most of your fingers and hand below the turtle, where it cannot reach. For very large turtles, a slight modification of this grip is best. Instead of using one hand, both hands should be used. Rather than placing your fingers under the turtle, slip both hands into the areas between the top of the turtle's rear legs and the underside of its carapace, and then clamp your thumb down on the top surface of the carapace. This grip lets you hold the rear of the turtle's shell, keeps your hands away from the rear legs, and allows you to point the turtle's head away from you, preventing a bite.

Finally, a word of caution: remember to clean your hands with soapy water after handling any turtles, and take care to clean off anything that you handle while your hands are dirty, especially anything that might come in contact with food. Some turtles may harbor bacteria that could cause salmonella or similar illnesses. These bacteria are a normal part of the turtle's intestinal flora and fauna, just as humans carry bacteria in their intestinal tract. With proper precautions and hygiene, these bacteria, if present, will not cause any problems. Anyone that is ill, the elderly, and very young children should also be cautious in handling turtles, as their immune systems may be weakened, which increases the chance of becoming infected.

All turtles, even baby ones like this common snapper, can carry salmonella. Always wash your hands after handling one.

Waste Management
Just like all animals, turtles eat food, extract what they need from it, and then expel the waste. Unfortunately, they usually do this in the water in which they live. If the water is not cleaned, it will quickly become fouled, from both uneaten food particles and from excrement. In addition to looking and smelling bad, fouled water will cause health problems for the turtle. For

these reasons, appropriate management of waste is one of the most important concerns for the turtle keeper.

One very effective method for dealing with waste in the turtle tank is to prevent its appearance in the first place. A majority of the normal amount of waste material can be eliminated or greatly reduced by feeding the turtles outside of their enclosure. To do this, simply fill a plastic container with water (cat litter trays work well for small- or medium-sized turtles, for example), place the food into it, and then put the turtle in the container. After the turtle has consumed all the food it is interested in eating, put the turtle back in its enclosure and dispose of the dirty water. In addition to the elimination of food debris, this method also helps reduce fecal material in the enclosure, as many chelonians will defecate just prior to or immediately after feeding.

An added benefit of exterior feeding is that it allows you to monitor the food intake of each turtle, and, at the same time, keep a check on the relative health of the chelonians. Feeding the animals outside the main aquarium does not guarantee clean water; you will still need to use filters or periodic water changes to reduce the amount of waste material in the captive environment.

Hygiene Reminder

Always wash your hands after handling your turtle or handling anything in the turtle tank. Until you can wash your hands, avoid handling food, rubbing your eyes, or putting you fingers in your mouth. Never eat or drink while handling your turtle or cleaning its enclosure.

Water Filtration Filtration of the water is a necessity for most aquatic turtle setups. A number of different types of filtering systems have been developed for use with turtles. These are usually adaptations of systems used with fish. In general, the main types are some form of a canister filter or undergravel filter. Canister filters are self-contained units holding material designed to remove particles of debris. Water is forced through the material by a pump and then returned to the tank. Undergravel filters use the gravel lining the bottom of the tank as an initial filter, pulling water through the gravel and then through an underlying plastic meshwork. Both types rely on both mechanical filtration and biological breakdown of the waste material to purify the water.

Canister filters, either submerged or placed outside the tank, generally work well. For smaller tanks, I prefer the fully submersible types that do not require an air pump, but are self-contained units, sucking water in through the bottom, passing it through various filters, and

Aquatic turtles will quickly foul their water, so frequent cleanings are a must. These spotted turtles are due for a water change.

expelling it out the top. For larger aquaria, stand-alone canister filters are a good investment. Although their initial cost can be high, the time saved in water and filter changes makes them well worth the money. Many different models are available from a number of different manufacturers. As with turtle tanks, larger is usually better. The greater the volume of water moved and the larger the filtering surface, the cleaner the water will remain. This will reduce the frequency of water changes required. Many turtle enthusiasts construct their own canister-style filtration systems using parts from garden ponds or even swimming pools. One word of caution: make sure you consider the rate of water exchange with the filtering system you intend to use when you are constructing the turtle tank. Some species of turtle prefer still or slow-moving water and may suffer if placed in a setup with a high volume of water flow.

Undergravel filters can be used, but often become clogged too quickly due to the large amount of waste material that turtles are capable of producing. Because undergravel filters rely on the gravel layer, the turtles themselves may interfere with proper filtration as they dig around in it. For these reasons, canister filters are more commonly used with turtles.

Even the best of filtration systems will occasionally require partial or complete changes of the water. A good practice is to set up a routine schedule for periodic partial water changes. If you have more than one turtle tank, you can change the water on a rotating basis to more evenly distribute the workload. Partial water changes are generally better than complete changes.

The method used to change the water will depend on the type of turtle tank that you have set up. Small plastic tubs or aquaria can be moved to a utility sink, emptied of decoration, and drained. However, this method does not work well for most turtle tanks. Instead, many keepers rely on hoses and siphons. One type of siphon attaches to the end of a faucet. The water from the faucet rushes through a stiff plastic tube. A hose is attached at the midpoint of the tube at a right angle to the flow of the water. The rushing water creates a vacuum in the hose, and if the far end of the hose is placed into the turtle tank, the vacuum will draw up the water and send it through the hose until it is dumped into the sink along with the faucet water. Once the tank is emptied, the water from the faucet can be diverted to go through the hose and fill up the tank again. Siphons like this are an invaluable aid in the fight to keep the turtle's home clean and healthy.

Some turtles may be intolerant of the difference between the aged water they're accustomed to and the new water that they're given. This can be especially problematic with certain species of turtle with specific needs based on their native environment. For example, the South American matamata, which routinely lives in water that is mildly acidic and soft, may not thrive on neutral or basic pH water with a lot of dissolved minerals.

Other turtles require additives in their water. The exact type of water used will be dependent on the turtle species—this is another reason why it is essential to have accurate information about the turtles that you keep. For those turtles that are particularly sensitive to changes in their water, exchanging only part of the water in the tank may ease the transition, as will the use of "aged" water. Kits that allow you to

Turtles and pH

Water can be acidic, neutral, or basic, depending on the amount of hydrogen ions present in it. The pH scale ranges from very acidic (a reading of 1), to neutral (7), to very basic (14). Most tap water in the United States is mildly basic (a pH range from 7 to 8). Unless you know that your turtles require basic or acidic water, you can use aged tap water with a neutral pH.

Mississippi map turtles and the other maps thrive only in clean water. Filtration is highly recommended for these species.

measure the hardness and pH of the water are available at most pet stores. These are very useful, especially if you are keeping an exotic turtle or one with specific mineral or pH requirements.

Feeding

Turtles will eat many different types of food, depending on the species and what is available in the local environment. Some turtles are almost entirely carnivorous, feeding on aquatic insects, snails, clams, fish, worms, crustaceans, and possibly amphibians. Some have special adaptations that help them capture prey items. For example, the alligator snapping turtle (*Macroclemys temminckii*) has a small tentacle in its mouth that looks remarkably like a worm, and the turtle uses this as a lure to attract fish.

Some species are primarily vegetarian. Common items for these turtles are various types of lettuces such as romaine or red-leaf (avoid iceberg), collard greens, and finely chopped mixed vegetables. Other species are omnivores that will eat whatever is abundant and easily obtained. This means that, for these turtles, food items will vary widely depending on the local environment. Also, if other turtles are present, competition for food items may alter what the turtles will consume. For example, studies in Belize with three species of mud turtle (*Kinosternon leucostomum*, *K. scorpioides*, and *Staurotypus triporcatus*) and a slider (*Trachemys scripta*) showed that diets altered as relative densities of turtles changed. The diets of different species are discussed in Chapter 6.

Variety of Foods

A variety in food items means that you should be familiar with the types of food normally consumed by the turtles that you keep. In captivity, turtles will eat many of the items that they feed on in their natural habitats if they are provided. Many will eagerly consume various insects, earthworms, small feeder guppies, raw beef heart, cooked chicken, prekilled pinky mice, or a low-fat dog food. For those species that are omnivorous, vegetable matter should also be offered on a routine basis. For vegetarian species, provide a changing mix of items from the produce department, especially leafy greens such as romaine, collards, dandelions, parsley, and rapini.

Many aquatic turtles relish earthworms. A young midland smooth softshell is shown.

Above all, remember to provide a varied diet. While individual turtles will often demonstrate a preference for a specific food, they should not be allowed to become fixated on one particular thing; items should be varied in order to provide a complete and balanced diet.

Supplements

Many turtle keepers supplement their turtles' diets with commercial turtle foods and trout chows. These turtle pellets will be accepted by most turtles, although it may take a period of acclimation. Commercial foods are fortified with vitamins and minerals that are required for a turtle's long-term health. Because of this, providing these pellets as a part of the meal is a good practice. I have successfully raised hatchlings of a number of species on a

Aged Water

Water that has been allowed to sit out for a few days (aged water) may help turtles that are sensitive to the condition of their water, as the aging allows time for chlorine in the water to evaporate into the air.

Carnivorous turtles, like this alligator snapper, are often fed live fish in captivity.

diet of commercial turtle pellets supplemented with live prey or vegetables, depending on the species. Most pet stores stock at least one brand of commercial food and will happily special order others. A number of online pet stores also carry these foods.

If a well-balanced diet is provided, most turtles, especially adults, will not require a lot of additional vitamin supplementation. However, periodic supplementation with vitamins and calcium may help prevent deficiencies due to undetected inadequacies in diet, even in turtles that routinely consume commercial turtle pellets. Unfortunately, it can be difficult to provide these supplements. Most semi-aquatic turtles eat in the water, where added powdered vitamins and minerals will wash off quickly. One easy means of providing more calcium and vitamins is in the form of a calcium block. Captive turtles in my collection are fond of these blocks, which are made of plaster of paris and added vitamin and calcium powder. Calcium carbonate, in the form of plaster of paris, is mixed with water, poured into molds, and allowed to solidify. A vitamin powder can be added while the plaster of paris is still liquid. Art supply stores are a good source of plaster of paris. Before purchasing it, check the ingredients list to verify that no anti-fungal compounds have been added to prevent the growth of mold or mildew.

Feeding Frenzy

A note of caution: Some of the more aggressive species have been known to bite at cagemates during feeding, sometimes leading to loss of limbs. If you opt to feed turtles together in the same tank, be aware of this potential problem and watch your turtles carefully while they are feeding.

These compounds can hurt turtles if they consume them. In addition to the benefits from calcium and vitamins, the blocks also help keep a turtle's jaws worn down. They are particularly helpful with rapidly growing hatchlings and any female turtles that might be producing eggs because they will benefit from the additional nutrients.

Feeding Schedule

Adult turtles do not require daily feeding. They should be fed as much as they will eat in a few minutes, once every second or third day. Do not overfeed your turtles. They will overeat and become fat, with the same consequences to their health as with any other overweight animal. Fat turtles can be recognized by their inability to retract their head and legs fully, or not all at the same time. Hatchlings and small juveniles can be fed daily until their growth rate begins to slow down.

Feed your animals individually in a separate container (plastic tubs or deep trays work well) because turtles can be rather messy eaters. When you feed them in their aquarium, broken up bits of food will quickly foul the water, forcing a water change every couple of days. If you have more than one turtle in a tank, individual feeding also allows you to monitor each turtle's eating habits to ensure that each turtle is getting the proper amount of food and nutrition.

Diet at a Glance

Below is a list of some of the most common turtles and what general type of diet they need. For more information, see the description of the species in Chapter 6. In many species, the juveniles are more carnivorous than the adults.

cooters	herbivorous
mud and musk turtles	omnivorous
painted turtle	omnivorous
red-bellied turtle	herbivorous
red-eared slider	omnivorous
Reeves' turtle	omnivorous
snappers	carnivorous
softshells	carnivorous

Chapter 4

Health Issues

Once a turtle has been established in captivity, health care falls into three major categories: dietary considerations, prevention of incidental infections, and treatment of injuries. Many of these problems can be prevented, or at least reduced, by a careful monitoring of your turtle's overall health. This section discusses the health issues that are commonly encountered by turtle keepers and gives practical suggestions for dealing with these issues.

Quarantine

Newly arrived turtles must be quarantined (even if they were captive-born and raised) if you already have turtles or obtain your turtles from two different sources. Quarantine is keeping the new arrival in a separate cage (and preferably room) until you are sure it is healthy. A month of quarantine is recommended; longer is always better. Without quarantine, whole collections can be wiped out through the introduction of a novel disease or parasite to which the older chelonians have no resistance.

Even captive-bred turtles should be quarantined. A hatchling pastel red-eared slider is pictured here.

The stress and debilitating conditions suffered by turtles during capture or transport can lead to a potentially fatal buildup of internal parasites, especially if they have been grossly mishandled. All newly acquired turtles should be examined immediately upon arrival, quarantined, and treated as needed.

Routine Inspection

Your turtle-keeping routine should include a few moments of inspection daily or every other day. This routine accomplishes a number of important things. First, you quickly become accustomed to the normal appearance and behavior of your turtle. Second, most turtles will become accustomed to being handled by you and should eventually remain calm when picked up. Finally, the inspection will reveal most potential problems, illnesses, or injuries. Health issues are more easily addressed if they are noticed early, while the turtle is still relatively healthy, than if they go undetected until they have advanced into potentially life-threatening problems. If you feed your turtle in a separate tub (as discussed in the section on feeding), you can perform this inspection while moving the turtle from its tank to its feeding tub.

Shell Examine the carapace and the plastron carefully. Inspect the edges of each scute, and make sure that they are not becoming loose. Many types of aquatic turtles routinely shed the very thin uppermost layer of each scute as they grow. However, it is not normal for many layers to dislodge at one time. If this happens, it may signal that there is an infection under the scute that is causing the layers to separate from the underlying bone. Often such infections will leave a layer of creamy material that looks vaguely like cottage cheese or toothpaste under the edge of the scute. This material can be squeezed out with mild pressure. Infections of this type often result when the turtle has too little basking time or too much bacteria builds up in the turtle's water area. More frequent water changes, in combination with increased basking time for the turtle, may halt the infection, but if it persists a veterinarian should be consulted.

If multiple turtles are kept together, you may see bite marks on the shell of one or more of the individuals. Occasionally, one aggressive turtle will repeatedly bite at the edges of the shells of its cagemates and may eventually chew pieces off of the shell. This problem also arises during the mating season if the male turtle is overly aggressive while courting the female. If this happens, the turtles should be immediately separated. The wounded area of the shell should be dried and disinfected. Iodine solution can be spread on the area with a cotton swab. The wound should be carefully watched to make sure that it doesn't become infected. If the damage is extensive, a vet should be consulted.

Limbs During the inspection, look at all of the turtle's legs and tail to make sure that there are no cuts or abrasions. Loose skin is not uncommon—turtles shed their old skin, but unlike snakes the skin comes off in small patches. As with the scutes, only a single layer should come off at one time. Skin shedding is more noticeable in some species than in others.

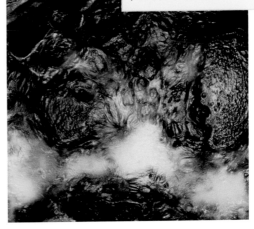

Shell rot in a painted turtle. Clean water and a suitable basking area should prevent this problem.

Head and Neck Finally, observe the turtle's head and neck. The turtle should have bright, shiny eyes that follow movements readily. There should be no irregular lumps on the neck or shoulders. The inside of the mouth should be a healthy color, usually pink, and not pale. Similarly, there should be no thick deposits lining the mouth. As with the scutes, this is a sign of an infection and usually requires veterinary assistance and medication to clear it up.

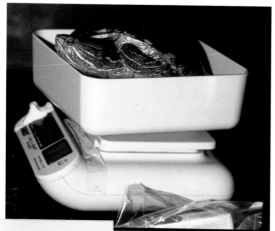
Weighing your turtle regularly is a good practice to adopt. A red-eared slider is shown.

Weight Regular weighing of your turtles is a good habit to adopt. A loss of weight is an early indicator that there is a health issue, so the turtle's weight should be monitored. An easy way to remember to do this is to add it to a routine task, such as when you do a complete water change. While the turtles are away from the water and dry, plop them on a kitchen scale and record their weight in a notebook. From this record you can quickly see if there is a problem. Larger turtles may need a large kitchen scale. Bathroom scales are usually not appropriate, as they are not accurate at the low end of their range, where the weight of most common turtles will tend to fall. Snapping turtles are the exception to this, but a snapper big enough to require a bathroom scale is not a turtle that very many people will be able to house successfully!

The easiest way to successfully weigh a turtle is with the help of a plastic tub or bucket that is larger than the turtle to be weighed. First place the tub on the scale and take note of its weight. Put the turtle inside the tub and weigh them both together. Then subtract the weight of the tub from the combined weight to determine the actual weight of the turtle. The tub will prevent the turtle from launching itself from the scale, which will allow you to get an accurate weight.

Dietary Problems

A major source of illness in turtles in captivity is an incomplete or inappropriate diet. Do not allow a turtle to become fixated on one food item; instead, make sure you offer a variety of foods to the animal. For example, even turtles who are carnivorous will occasionally take some plant matter. It is also helpful to periodically supplement the animal's diet with vitamins and calcium, usually in the form of a powder sprinkled on food or a liquid injected into a favorite prey item. The calcium block mentioned in the section on feeding can also be used to deliver needed vitamins and minerals, if they are added to the plaster of paris before the block solidifies.

Calcium powders and vitamins for reptiles are available at most pet stores. Check the ingredient list on any of these products to confirm that they contain vitamin D3 and vitamin A. Deficiencies in these two vitamins are the most commonly seen dietary problems in turtles.

Vitamin D3 is made in the body when the skin is exposed to certain wavelengths of ultraviolet radiation (found naturally in sunlight). Turtles kept indoors usually have no exposure to unfiltered sunlight, so they require supplemental vitamin D3, which is necessary for proper bone development and maintenance. Turtles lacking vitamin D3 develop metabolic bone disease, which is often characterized by a distorted shell, leg problems, and softening of the jaws.

Lethal Medications

One drug that is commonly used by veterinarians for other pets should never be given to your turtles—ivermectin. Ivermectin and related compounds are often prescribed for internal parasites such as heartworm in dogs. However, these drugs are lethal to turtles and tortoises. If your vet prescribes this drug for your turtle, find another vet, as she is not well-informed about turtle care!

Turtles lacking sufficient vitamin A develop swollen eyes and often have open sores on their skin. Diets containing fruits and vegetables with carotene, such as sweet potato or winter squash, will prevent vitamin A deficiency. Unfortunately, some turtle species will not eat these foods, and so an occasional vitamin supplement can be provided. Follow the instructions in the feeding section of Chapter 3.

Parasites and Infections

Incidental infections and parasite infestations can be avoided or eliminated by careful monitoring of the animals and their environment. This includes cleaning the aquarium at regular

Red-eared slider being treated for a fungal infection of the plastron.

intervals, water changes, and quarantine for any new or ill turtles. If parasites are found in fecal material or in the water of the tank, a veterinarian will need to be consulted to obtain the proper medication to eliminate the problem. Signs of an infection, such as bubbles from the turtle's nostrils, difficulty breathing, a sudden loss of appetite, or an inability to swim properly, should be taken seriously, and the turtle should be examined by a veterinarian familiar with reptiles.

Injuries

Injuries can occur because of improper cage design (sharp rocks, for example) or through aggressive interactions with other turtles. Frequent examinations of the turtles for injuries and prompt attention to any injuries discovered will prevent minor cuts and abrasions from becoming infected. You can clean wounds with diluted povidone iodine. Topical polysporin ointments also work well on minor injuries and have the advantage of being relatively water-insoluble. If the injury is extensive or the turtle does not respond quickly, a veterinarian should be consulted.

Gravid Females

Female turtles that are being bred or that are known to have mated require special care. They should receive a well-rounded diet, with increased supplementation of calcium. Also, the keeper must carefully note changes in behavior. Changes such as loss of appetite or

Finding a Herp Vet

It is not always easy to find vets who are experienced with reptiles and amphibians. Here are some suggestions to help you locate a vet who can help with your pet turtle. It is best if you locate one before you actually have an emergency

- Call veterinarians listed as "exotic" or "reptile" vets in the phonebook. Ask them questions to be sure they are familiar with aquatic turtles.
- Ask at your local pet stores, zoos, herpetological societies, and animal shelters to see if there is someone they can recommend.
- Contact the Association of Reptilian and Amphibian Veterinarians. Their website is www.arav.org.

restlessness in females known or suspected to be carrying eggs should serve as a warning signal to keepers. For example, if the enclosure is unsuitable for nest construction or incubation, a female turtle may retain her eggs rather than lay them in an area that does not suit her.

Female turtles with eggs are usually restless and will wander around their enclosure occasionally pawing at the dirt. If this habit persists, it means that the female is not happy with any of the egg-laying sites. She may choose to lay her eggs on the surface, where they are usually destroyed accidentally or even eaten by other turtles in the enclosure. Alternatively she may refuse to lay the eggs. After a while, she may have problems moving her back legs, and stop walking or swimming. The retained eggs can sometimes be felt in the turtle's body cavity by gently probing inward with your fingers from both sides in the rear leg cavities. Unfortunately, retained eggs can lead to health complications, especially if an egg ruptures or becomes over-calcified. If you suspect your female is egg bound, seek immediate veterinary care.

Leeches

Some wild-caught turtles will arrive harboring leeches. These parasites are a normal consequence of living outdoors, but they should be removed from the turtle. A few drops of rubbing alcohol will cause the leech to drop off, and the area of the bite can then be cleaned and disinfected.

Veterinary Care

While turtle keepers can perform a lot of basic first aid for turtles, the experience of a good veterinarian may be necessary, depending on the situation. Unfortunately, vets with experience in reptile care are not common. Seeking out and cultivating a relationship with a good reptile vet is one of the best things that a novice turtle keeper can do. Local herpetological societies can be the best source of advice for veterinary aid, as the members of the society have already done a lot of the background research needed to identify those veterinarians that are best qualified to treat reptiles.

Finally, the best time to locate a qualified vet is before one is needed, rather than when your turtle is sick or injured. If at all possible, take your turtle to the vet when it is healthy. This kind of checkup gives the vet a chance to examine the turtle, determine that it is healthy, and provides him or her with a comparison for those times when the turtle is ill or injured. The help of a good reptile vet is an essential ingredient in the long-term success of turtle keeping.

Chapter 5

Breeding

There are a number of questions that you will need to address and preparations that you will need to make if you decide that you want to breed turtles. This section will outline some of the considerations necessary for successful breeding. If you do attempt to breed your turtles, don't be discouraged by the amount of information that you'll need to review to adequately address these questions. While not every keeper wants to breed their animals, or should even consider it, successful breeding is a very strong indication that you are providing the proper environment for them. Also, if more captive-born turtles are available, fewer turtles will be taken from the wild for the pet trade.

The Minimum

There is only one absolute requirement for successful breeding: a male and female of the same species. All other factors may or may not be necessary, depending on the species, keeping conditions, and the individual turtles themselves.

Breeding Basics

In order to be successful in breeding your turtles, the first step is to obtain a male and a female of the same species. While this step may seem obvious, it can be more difficult than you might expect. If you already have one or more turtles, can you accurately determine the sex? If you only have a single turtle, do you know enough about it that you can be sure that you can obtain more of the same species or subspecies of the opposite sex?

Once you have obtained a pair of turtles, do you know enough about the natural history of your turtles that you're confident that you are providing an environment that is suitable for mating and egg-laying? If you overcome these hurdles and your turtles lay a clutch of eggs, do you know how to care for the eggs to ensure that they will hatch?

If you decide that you want to breed turtles before you acquire any animals, attempt to obtain turtles of known sex from the same source. If the turtles are wild caught, obtaining them at the same time and from the same place increases the likelihood that they were captured together, and therefore will be the same species or subspecies. Alternatively, research the turtles you wish to breed and learn how to distinguish them from similar species. Unfortunately, sometimes you will not be able to directly observe the turtles before you purchase them—for example, if you obtain your turtles through an online dealer. Attending a national or regional reptile show may be the best solution.

Sexing

The sex of a turtle can be difficult to determine, but there are a few guidelines that apply to

Male turtles (left) have longer and thicker tails than the females (right). In musk turtles and some other species, the males also have a concave plastron, while the females have a flat one.

most turtles. The location of the cloacal opening (also called the vent) on the turtle's tail is the best indication of its sex. Hold the turtle vertically, with the bottom plastron facing you. Lightly extend the tail so that it is pointing straight down. Examine the location of the opening in comparison to the edge of the upper shell. The opening will be past the edge of the carapace for males, while for females the vent will be much closer to the body of the turtle, occurring before the edge of the carapace. This inspection is only accurate for adult turtles. Juvenile turtles may not yet exhibit a difference in location, and so you may misidentify the turtle's sex. When checking the sex in this manner, keep in mind the adult size of the species you are examining, as size is usually the best indication that adulthood has been reached.

Turtles from northern areas, like this eastern spiny softshell, usually must go through a hibernation period before breeding.

Male turtles will occasionally extend their penises, especially during the breeding season, upon being placed into the water after handling or sometimes during handling. Some keepers upon seeing this behavior for the first time become rather alarmed and worried that the turtle is suffering from some type of intestinal prolapse. The turtle will usually rapidly retract his penis if disturbed, while an animal suffering from a prolapse will not be able to do so. Observing a turtle extruding his penis is, of course, a very good indication of the sex of that particular turtle.

Some turtles exhibit secondary sexual characteristics, just as humans do. Some species have differing skin or shell colorations between the sexes. Often, female and male turtles will grow to different final sizes, with the males usually being smaller than the females. For example, in most map turtle species, the female can reach a foot in length, while males of the same species are mature at approximately a third of that size. In the red-eared slider, the males develop very long, curved claws on their front feet. As part of their mating ritual, they will swim backwards in front of another turtle and attempt to stroke its cheeks with these claws. While this behavior, and the presence of the long claws, identifies that turtle as male, the other turtle may not necessarily be female; at the height of the breeding season, males will court other males if there are no females present. Male turtles often have a slight depression in the center of their plastron, while the female plastron is usually flat. The depression in the male plastron allows the male to fit more closely to the female's curved carapace during mating.

Hibernation

Some turtle populations hibernate during the winter months. Turtles from areas of the world that experience winters during which the temperature drops below freezing are likely to spend a portion of the winter buried in the mud underwater or at the water's edge. So, if you keep a turtle from one of these populations, should you provide a hibernation period for your turtle? The answer to this question is not a simple one.

The chief problem with hibernating turtles in captivity is doing it in a manner that induces true hibernation without posing a danger to the turtle. In the wild, the turtle is able to select an appropriate location for hibernation. This location will allow the turtle to enter a dormant state in which its metabolic rate slows down, while also preventing it from getting so cold that it freezes. In captivity, the turtle is absolutely dependent on the keeper to achieve this balance. If the hibernation area is too warm, the turtle will use up all of its energy stores and starve to death, but if it is too cold, the turtle will freeze to death. For aquatic turtles, the proper moisture levels must also be maintained or else the turtle will become dehydrated, a potentially lethal problem.

Hibernation has been thought to be necessary for optimal health and breeding success for a number of types of reptile, including turtles. However, this idea has been a point of disagreement for years. For example, for turtles with a wide range (such as sliders or cooters), animals from the southern portion of the range do not hibernate, while those in the northern reaches are required to hibernate by the local conditions. Thus, while these types of turtle are fully capable of hibernating, they do not do so unless the local environment forces it upon them.

If you are keeping a wild-caught turtle that you know was obtained from a region that has cold winters and you wish to breed the turtle, you can consider the possibility of hibernating it. However, if your turtle is captive bred or is from a southern population or species, hibernation is not necessary. Also, only turtles that are in excellent health should be hibernated—if a turtle shows any signs of illness, do not attempt to hibernate it. Hibernating a sick or underweight turtle can result in the death of the turtle. Finally, juvenile turtles are not good candidates for hibernation; only adults should be hibernated.

Most species of aquatic turtles mate in the water. A pair of Texas map turtles is shown, with a softshell spectator.

In order to successfully hibernate a turtle, the following steps should be taken:

1. Beginning a couple of weeks prior to hibernation, provide a fasting period, as the turtle should have no food in its digestive tract when it begins hibernation.

2. Cool the turtle down, over a period of a few days to a week, to a temperature of approximately 40°F (4.4°C). Temperatures below freezing will kill the turtle, while temperatures above 45°-50°F (7.2°-10°C) will not induce a hibernation state.

3. Monitor the status of the turtle carefully during the hibernation period, but take care to keep the turtle at the proper temperature.

4. Hibernation times can vary, but need not extend for more than six to eight weeks, even in areas that experience a long winter. To avoid a shock to the hibernating turtle's system, it is better to warm the turtle slowly, over the period of a day or two.

To hibernate a turtle indoors, an area that can be maintained at 40°F (4.4°C) is required Most people keep their houses, even their basements, at temperatures that are too high for hibernation. A small temperature-controlled refrigerator can be used for hibernation. Care must taken to ensure that the temperature range inside of it does not fluctuate and that there is an adequate supply of fresh air. Before attempting hibernation, monitor the temperature in the refrigerator carefully for a week or so, checking it a few times a day with

Brumation

Herpetologists often use the term *brumation*, rather than hibernation, because there are significant differences between reptiles and mammals in the way in which they become dormant during periods of cold. Hibernation is considered a more complete state of torpor than brumation.

a very accurate thermometer to ensure that an appropriate temperature can be maintained.

Once you are ready to hibernate your turtle, place it in a tub half-filled with water. Cover the tub with a lid that has holes in it for air exchange, and place it in the refrigerator. Air quality in the refrigerator can be maintained by opening the door once a day. Ventilation can also be provided by inserting a couple of rigid hollow tubes through the door seal or other portions of the refrigerator. At least two tubes, one at the top and one at the bottom, are required to allow for proper air flow.

For turtles being kept outdoors in a pond, hibernation may occur naturally if the pond is sufficiently deep that it will not freeze solid during the winter and if the bottom is covered in mud into which the turtle can burrow. Shallow artificial ponds are not suitable for hibernating turtles.

Turtle Mating Behaviors

Turtles exhibit specific behaviors during mating. These behaviors can differ from species to species, but some are relatively common. Courtship can involve head bobbing, nipping at back legs or the edges of the carapace, chases, and other ritualistic movements, some of which can be quite complex. For example, a male red-eared slider will follow a female for a while, then rapidly swim around in front of her and turn around to face her. He then strokes both sides of her face and neck with his very long, sword-like front claws. After a few moments of stroking, he will then attempt to mount her. If she is unreceptive, he will begin the ritual again.

Mud turtles exhibit mating behaviors that are typical of many other species of turtle. In general, they do not have an elaborate courtship procedure, although there are a number of variations among the different species. Typical events include a phase where the male follows the female, sniffing at her cloaca and sometimes at the bridge between the carapace and plastron. This is occasionally accompanied by a head-to-head confrontation or nudging by the male. If the female moves away, the male will give chase, repeating the sniffing and nudging until the female remains stationary. The male then mounts the female from the side or rear, using all four feet to grasp the shell.

When actual copulation takes place, the male may move backward or up at an angle to the female's carapace. These motions can depend on the relative size of the individual turtles and on the specific species involved, since tail length and location of the vents may contribute to positioning.

Turtle mating can be a very aggressive act. Injuries, such as bites to the limbs or shell, are not uncommon. In some species, male-to-male battles occur prior to mating with females, and these battles can often lead to injury. However, there is evidence that these battles may be necessary for successful mating. If you are trying to breed your turtles, pay careful attention to their physical condition during the mating season, and remove any animal that is injured. In extreme cases, females have been drowned by an overly-aggressive male that does not allow the female to surface for a breath of air during mating.

Egg Laying and Incubation

Aquatic turtles require a land area in which to lay their eggs. If a female turtle is in a turtle tank that doesn't have a land area, she will retain her eggs as long as she can, and then lay them in the water. The eggs will quickly drown if they are not rescued, or they will be consumed by other turtles in the tank. Also, if the female holds onto her eggs for too long, they can become over-calcified, which can lead to difficulties when she does try to lay them. Female turtles have been known to die from being egg bound.

Suitable land areas are not hard to construct in outdoor turtle enclosures, and it is a good idea to provide several areas from which the turtle can choose. Each area should receive some direct sunlight during the day. The soil should be loose and slightly damp, but not wet. For indoor enclosures, a suitable land area will need to be built into the turtle tank. It should be larger than the turtle, so that she can safely turn around and find an appropriate

Softshell eggs in the nest.

position for laying her eggs. The female will dig out a hole with her back legs, lay the eggs at the bottom of the hole, and then cover them up.

The number of eggs varies considerably, depending on the species of turtle and the female's age. Small turtles may lay only a few, while large turtles may lay dozens of eggs. If you don't observe the eggs being laid, you may not realize that she has laid them. If the area in which she deposited the eggs has a suitable temperature and is kept moist, they may hatch where they were placed. This, however, may be risky for the hatchlings, as the adult turtles may consider them to be a tasty snack. It is better to rescue the eggs from the land area, and incubate them in a separate container. Dig the eggs out of the soil slowly and carefully. Do not turn them when moving them to the incubation container.

Incubation

Turtle eggs, unlike the eggs of birds, do not need to be rotated and flipped periodically. In fact, doing so will lead to the death of the developing turtle. Instead, the eggs should be left undisturbed in a container that provides the appropriate level of moisture. If the eggs were fertile, the moisture level correct, and the temperature falls within the

Get Ready to Incubate

It is recommended that you have the incubator set up for at least several days before you think you will need it. By doing this, you can make sure the incubator is holding the correct temperature without exposing the eggs to temperature fluctuations while you adjust the thermostat. Also, if your turtle happens to lay eggs earlier than predicted, you will be ready.

right range, the turtle embryos within the eggs should develop properly and hatch on their own, with little intervention required on the part of the turtle keeper.

There are many different approaches to incubating turtle eggs. One of the most basic methods is to partially bury the eggs in a substrate that provides the right amount of moisture. Even though turtle eggs are hard-shelled, they can still dehydrate over time if the surrounding environment is too dry. The opposite is also true—eggs can drown if placed in too much water. Many keepers put turtle eggs in dirt in plastic containers, with approximately one-quarter of the egg still visible. Often the dirt is a mix of potting soil and absorbent material, such vermiculite, peat or sphagnum moss, although some breeders use only vermiculite. The use of sand alone should be avoided, as it tends to compact and harden over time, fatally trapping hatchlings within their eggs. The container should not be completely closed up, in order to provide a supply of oxygen to the developing embryos. Some keepers and institutions that produce a large number of turtle eggs each year rely on incubators that maintain a particular humidity level and temperature range, but the use of these devices isn't necessary for successful egg incubation.

The egg of a peninsula cooter incubating in vermiculite, which is commonly used for this purpose by reptile breeders.

Temperature-dependant Sex Determination The eggs need to be incubated at a fairly warm temperature—approximately 28°C (80°F) is commonly used. However, the temperature at which turtle eggs are incubated can have a profound effect on the eggs. In some turtle species, the sex of the hatchling is determined by their chromosomes, as in humans. Other turtle species exhibit a phenomenon known as temperature-dependent sex determination, commonly abbreviated as TSD. Turtle eggs that are incubated at a particular temperature hatch out turtles that have a particular sex. In other words, the temperature that the egg experiences determines the sex of the turtle within the egg. Different species of turtles exhibit variations of TSD. In many species, males are produced at lower temperatures, while females predominate at higher temperatures, and a mix of males and females is seen at intermediate temperatures. Other strategies are possible. For mud turtles, eggs incubated at an intermediate

Table 2. Effects of Incubation Temperature on the Sex of the Hatchlings in Several Species of Turtle.

Turtle	Cool Incubation	Intermediate	Warm Incubation
Red-eared Slider	male	male	female
Map Turtle	male	male	female
Painted Turtle	male	male	female
Red-bellied Turtle	male	male	female
Spotted Turtle	male	male	female
Mud Turtle	female	male	female
Musk Turtle	female	male	female
Alligator Snapping Turtle	female	male	female
African Mud Turtle	female	male	female
Softshell turtles	equal	equal	equal

Notes:
Cool Incubation is 75°F (24°C) and lower; **Intermediate** is between 76 and 81°F (24.4 – 27.2°C); **Warm Incubation** is above 86°F (30°C).

Softshell turtles are shown for comparison; these turtles do not exhibit TSD.

The information in this table was adapted from "Sex Determination in Turtles: Diverse Patterns and Some Possible Adaptive Values" by Michael A. Ewert and Craig E. Nelson, *Copeia* 199: 50-69 (1991).

temperature range give predominantly male turtles, while females are produced at temperatures above or below this temperature interval. Thus, choosing a temperature to incubate any turtle eggs is an important decision and should be made based on the particular type of turtle that you have. The table shows the patterns of TSD exhibited by a number of the turtle species discussed in this book.

Incubation Time

Incubation times range widely between different types of turtles. Two months is usually a minimum time from egg laying to hatching, but depending on the type of turtle and various environmental conditions, incubation times can range up to seven or eight months, even lasting over a winter.

Hatching

When the turtle is ready to hatch, it uses a specialized "egg-tooth," located on the tip of its nose, to chip a small hole in the end of the egg, and then uses its legs and head to crack open the egg completely. Upon emergence from the egg, the baby turtle is often rather cylindrical in shape, conforming to the shape of the egg itself. A remnant of the yolk sac that nourished it during development can usually be seen on the plastron of the turtle; this sac usually disappears or falls off after a short time.

Care of Hatchlings

Newly hatched turtles are capable of swimming and eating. They should be placed in a smaller version of the adults' turtle tank. A small plastic tub with a sloping rock is usually an appropriate container for hatchlings. Hatchlings should be fed regularly with a variety of food sources. They benefit from exposure to natural sunlight, as it helps stimulate the production of necessary vitamins. Provide the baby turtles with a source of calcium (such as the calcium block described earlier), as their actively growing bones require it. With the proper food and care, hatchlings will grow very rapidly in their first year of life.

No Filter for Babies

Using a filter in a hatchling turtle enclosure is not recommended. The water flow from a filter is usually stronger than hatchling turtles can safely handle. Instead, water changes should be made more frequently, as the water becomes fouled from fecal material and uneaten food.

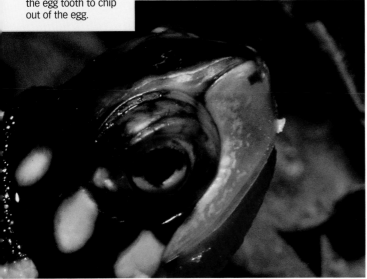

The small white projection on the face of this hatchling spotted turtle is the egg tooth. Turtles use the egg tooth to chip out of the egg.

However, take care not to overfeed them or their growth may be too rapid, which can usually be seen as shell abnormalities. The young turtles will need to be moved to larger tanks periodically as they grow. These tanks can include a filtration system once the turtles become strong enough to resist the flow of water these systems produce.

Chapter 6

Species Descriptions

Without proper care, a turtle will not survive and prosper in captivity. However, equally important for successful turtle keeping is the selection of an appropriate turtle. An often overlooked part of keeping a turtle as a pet is an understanding of the requirements of the specific species that you have selected. Some turtles are easier to keep in captivity than others, depending on how readily they adjust to a captive environment and the presence of people. True success in keeping turtles starts with choosing the correct one for your particular circumstances. This chapter provides information on the natural history of common turtles, allowing potential owners to make informed decisions as to which turtle, they wish to keep. Information is provided on a number of species that are not suitable for beginning turtle keepers, but can be maintained successfully by experienced keepers who can meet their specialized needs.

Turtles are divided into two main groups—the cryptodiran (hidden-necked) and pleurodiran (side-necked) turtles. In practical terms, this distinction does not affect the decision as to which type of turtle to keep in captivity. No representatives of the side-necked group are found in North America, so any available turtles of this kind will be either imported or bred in captivity. Many of the side-necked turtles are fascinating animals and are no more difficult to maintain in captivity than cryptodiran turtles from North America, if healthy specimens are obtained. However, they often cost significantly more than North American species, and so many beginning turtle keepers opt for one of these. Rather than describe turtles based on their classification, this section describes the turtles based on their location (i.e. exotic or native to North America) and the degree of difficulty in keeping and breeding that group of turtles in captivity.

Red-eared sliders are bred in large numbers. Several color varieties, like this albino, are available in the hobby.

North American Species
Sliders, Cooters, and Red-Bellied Turtles
Species, Descriptions, and Range The most common turtle in captivity in the US is the red-eared slider (*Trachemys scripta elegans*). This greenish turtle, with a patterned carapace, green and yellow stripes on its face and limbs, and the distinguishing red "ear" blotch directly behind its eyes, is recognized immediately by most people. It is a medium to large turtle, with females reaching over a foot (30.5 cm) in length. Males are usually significantly smaller and can be identified by their very long front claws. Large numbers of red-eared sliders hatchlings are produced each year on turtle farms in the southern part of the US. Many of these hatchlings are sent across the country and even exported around the world. Because of this practice, red-eared sliders have become established in many different states outside their native range and also in many foreign countries including Great Britain, Japan, South Africa, and Korea.

In the US, the red-eared slider is naturally found in the south-central portion of the country in calm waterways, ponds, and lakes. The red-eared slider is one subspecies of slider; the other two subspecies that are found in the US are the yellow-bellied slider (*Trachemys scripta scripta*) and the Cumberland slider (*Trachemys scripta troostii*). The yellow-bellied slider differs from the red-eared slider in that it lacks the red ear and has a solid yellow plastron, unlike the red-eared slider, which has a dark splotch at the center of each scute on its plastron. The Cumberland slider has a yellow or orange blotch behind its eyes, rather than the red blotch of the red-eared slider.

In addition to the three subspecies of T. *scripta* in the US, there are up to four to five times as many subspecies ranging from Mexico and the Caribbean islands south into Columbia and Venezuela. These subspecies are quite variable in appearance and size, and many are very poorly known. There is also a second *Trachemys* species, the Big Bend slider (*Trachemys gaigeae*), which is found along the Rio Grande River in Texas.

A number of other turtle species superficially resemble the sliders; they are generally referred to as cooters or red-bellied turtles, depending on the species. These turtles look like heavier versions of the sliders, but generally with less markings on their shells and much fewer and thicker lines on the head and limbs. They fall into the genus *Pseudemys*, and seven

Table 3. Sliders, Cooters, Red-bellied, & Painted Turtles

Scientific Name	Common Name	Range
Trachemys scripta scripta	Yellow-bellied Slider	Southern Virginia to northern Florida
elegans	Red-eared Slider	The Mississippi River valley from Illinois south to the Gulf of Mexico
troostii	Cumberland Slider	Cumberland and Tennessee River valleys
Trachemys gaigeae	Big Bend Slider	The Rio Grande River in Texas and south into Mexico
Pseudemys concinna	River Cooter	Southern USA from Louisiana and Missouri to the East Coast
Pseudemys floridana	Florida Cooter	Florida north along the coast to the southern edge of Virginia
Pseudemys gorzugi	Rio Grande Cooter	Western Texas south into Mexico
Pseudemys texana	Texas River Cooter	Gulf coast into Central Texas
Pseudemys rubriventris	Red-bellied Turtle	Southern edge of Pennsylvania to North Carolina, also Massachusetts
Pseudemys nelsoni	Florida Red-bellied Turtle	Florida
Pseudemys alabamensis	Alabama Red-bellied Turtle	South-western corner of Alabama
Chrysemys picta picta	Eastern Painted Turtle	Atlantic coast from Canada to Georgia
marginata	Midland Painted Turtle	East of the Mississippi from Quebec and Ontario south to Tennessee
bellii	Western Painted Turtle	From Ontario west to Oregon, and south to Missouri and Colorado
dorsalis	Southern Painted Turtle	From Illinois and Missouri south to the Gulf of Mexico

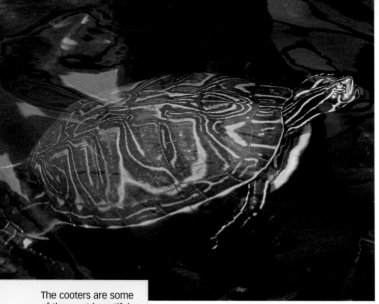

The cooters are some of the most beautiful of the North American aquatic turtles, as demonstrated by this peninsula cooter.

species occur within the US. The cooters are the river cooter (*Pseudemys concinna*), found from Louisiana and Missouri east; the Florida cooter (*P. floridana*), found in Florida and up the east coast to North Carolina; the Rio Grande cooter (*P. gorzugi*) and the Texas river cooter (*P. texana*), both of which are found in Texas.

The red-bellied turtles consist of three species. The common red-bellied turtle (*Pseudemys rubriventris*) ranges from Pennsylvania south to North Carolina, with an isolated population in Massachusetts. The other two species are the Florida red-bellied turtle (*P. nelsoni*) and the Alabama red-bellied turtle (*P. alabamensis*). As might be expected from their common names, these turtles all have a reddish-orange or reddish-yellow plastron. The cooters and red-bellied turtles grow slightly larger than the sliders and can reach sizes of 16-18 inches (40.6-45.7 cm) in the females of some species.

Natural History Sliders, cooters, and red-bellied turtles are found in most bodies of water within their range. They are avid baskers and prefer habitats that offer plenty of basking sites, such as fallen trees, offshore stumps, or rocks. The sliders are omnivorous, eating whatever is available and abundant. The cooters and red-bellied turtles are more herbivorous, although they will eat insects or meat on occasion. As with many other types of turtle, the juveniles are considerably more carnivorous than the adults; as they age, their dietary preferences slowly change.

Suitability As Pets Sliders, cooters, and red-bellied turtles are the species that are most likely to be encountered in a pet store. In fact, the red-eared slider is the single most common turtle in the pet trade and has been for decades. Their popularity in the pet trade is due to the fact that they are all relatively hardy, adapt well to captive maintenance, do not have difficult dietary needs, and are very attractive. Most of the individual turtles encountered in pet stores will be adult males, or juveniles of either sex, because of the 1975 federal law that prevents the sale of turtles under a length of 4 inches (10.2 cm).

The main drawback to these turtles is their maximum adult size—they often reach sizes that are larger than most novice turtle keepers expect or are prepared to handle. If, however, their size is taken into consideration, these turtles make an excellent choice for captive maintenance programs. Because so many of them are present in the pet trade, unwanted turtles often show up at animal rescue societies or in the adoption programs that herpetological societies run. Keepers that are interested in sliders or cooters should contact their local societies and inquire about potential adoptions.

Painted Turtles

Species, Descriptions, and Range The painted turtle (*Chrysemys picta*) is found almost exclusively in the US, ranging across the country and edging into Canada. There are four recognized subspecies within *C. picta*: the eastern painted turtle (*C. p. picta*), the midland painted turtle (*C. p. marginata*), the western painted turtle (*C. p. bellii*), and the southern painted turtle (*C. p. dorsalis*). Each subspecies is distinct and can be recognized both by appearance and by range. All are very attractive turtles, and their common name is well deserved.

The eastern painted turtle is found along the eastern seaboard. It has a glossy black carapace, often with red markings along the edge. The seams dividing each scute in the front-to-back rows line up from row to row in this subspecies; in other subspecies, the seams are staggered, rather than lining up. The plastron is a uniform yellow color, while the turtle's skin is a mix of thin yellow and red lines, separated by thicker black areas.

The midland painted turtle is found east of the Mississippi. While similar in appearance to the eastern painted, the midland painted turtle has staggered seams between its carapacial scutes, and its plastron has a dark region in the center.

The western painted turtle, which ranges across the US and lower Canada from the Midwest to Washington, is usually lighter in coloration than the other painted turtles, with its carapace tending more toward an olive color. It also has a darker

Rare Red-bellies

The Alabama red-bellied turtle and the common red-bellied turtles of Massachusetts are both so rare that they are listed as endangered under the Endangered Species Act. Please do not collect these species to be your pets.

The southern painted turtle is the only painted turtle with a stripe on its back.

central area on the plastron that is usually larger than in the midland painted turtle.

Finally, the southern painted turtle is found from Illinois and Missouri south to the Gulf Coast. It has a very distinctive stripe running down the center of its carapace and a solid yellow plastron.

The western painted turtle is the largest of the group—females, which grow larger than males, can reach almost a foot (30.5 cm) in length. The other three subspecies rarely reach half that size. The southern painted turtle usually grows to a final carapacial length of 5 inches (12.7 cm).

Natural History Painted turtles are predominantly found in slow-moving waters such as ponds, lakes, and slow streams. They are known for their tendency to bask. Often, dozens of painted turtles can be found on fallen tree trunks, with limbs extended to catch all of the sun's rays. These turtles usually bask in the morning, spend the midday foraging for food, and then either retire for the day or return to basking, depending on the time of year, the weather, and the ambient temperature. Northern populations are quite cold-resistant, and researchers have observed painted turtles moving under the ice of frozen streams and ponds. Turtles in the northern portion of their range usually hibernate, while southern populations may not.

Painted turtles are omnivorous, eating plant material or insects, snails, and occasionally fish, depending on availability. The diet of juvenile turtles is more heavily weighted toward insects, but this preference shifts as the turtle ages. In adults, the bulk of the diet is more likely to consist of plant material. Painted turtles are not considered to be aggressive, although there are occasional shoving matches over the best basking spots.

Suitability As Pets Painted turtles are remarkably similar to sliders and cooters in their environmental and dietary requirements. They adapt well to captivity if kept in clean, clear water and given adequate basking opportunities. As the more commonly available subspecies do not reach the same large size as sliders and cooters, they are quite well-suited for captive maintenance indoors. If only one turtle is going to be kept, a male is usually the better choice, as their adult size is smaller than that of a female. They are not as nervous in disposition as map turtles, but they are also not as calm as the sliders or cooters. Their small size, pleasant nature, and beautiful coloration make them a favorite turtle for both novice and advanced turtle keepers.

Mud and Musk Turtles

Species, Descriptions, and Range There are two subfamilies in the family Kinosternidae, the Staurotypinae and the Kinosterninae. Each subfamily has two genera (see the table for a list of species and subspecies and their common names). The Staurotypinae turtles, consisting of *Claudius* and *Staurotypus*, are found from central Mexico into northern Central America. The Kinosterninae consists of *Kinosternon* and *Sternotherus*. These turtles range more widely, occurring from southern Canada through much of South America.

The turtles in *Claudius* and *Staurotypus* are all moderately large musk turtles with three keels running the length of the carapace. The plastron is small and narrow, cruciform in shape, with seven or eight scutes. The genus *Claudius* contains only one turtle, *Claudius angustatus* the narrow-bridged musk turtle. The plastron of the narrow-bridged musk turtle has seven bones, unlike any other turtle. Another unique feature of *C. angustatus* is the presence of two cusps on the turtle's upper jaw.

Two species, *Staurotypus salvinii* and *Staurotypus triporcatus*, make up the genus *Staurotypus*. These turtles are the largest in the family: *S. salvinii* (the Pacific coast giant musk turtle) can reach a length of 10 inches (25.4 cm), while *S. triporcatus* (the Mexican giant musk turtle) grows to almost 16 inches (40.6 cm). *S. salvinii* can be distinguished from *S. triporcatus* by its smaller size and also by its wider and more flattened carapace. Both turtles can be distinguished from any other mud or musk turtle by their size.

The subfamily Kinosterninae is a much larger and more varied group than the Staurotypinae. Turtles in the Kinosterninae subfamily can be distinguished from Staurotypinae chelonians by the number of scutes on their plastrons, as turtles in the Kinosterninae have ten or eleven scutes, compared to the seven or eight in Staurotypinae. Another feature that differs is the absence of the entoplastral bone that is present in the

Staurotypinae, but this is not particularly useful when comparing living turtles.

The Kinosterninae subfamily is broken up into two genera. One genus is *Kinosternon* (mud turtles), which has at least fifteen species and a number of subspecies. The other genus is *Sternotherus* (musk turtles), with four species, one of which has two subspecies. Musk turtles are native to the US, with one species (*S. odoratus*) ranging up into Canada. Mud turtles are more widely dispersed, with species found from Connecticut (*K. subrubrum*) south through the southern and central portions of the US, through Mexico and Central America, and entering South America as far as northern Argentina (*K. scorpioides*).

The Mexican giant musk turtle is the largest species in the family. It has three distinct keels on its carapace.

Four species of *Sternotherus* are recognized. *Sternotherus carinatus*, the razor-backed musk turtle, deserves its name. This turtle has a very sharply sloping carapace; when viewed from the front, the turtle appears to be triangular. The plastron only has ten scutes, unlike the rest of the species of *Sternotherus* and *Kinosternon*. The flattened musk turtle, *S. depressus*, also is aptly named. Its carapace is very flattened and wide. The loggerhead musk turtle, *S. m. minor*, has a carapacial shape that is intermediate between *S. depressus* and *S. carinatus*. Like the rest of the genus, *S. minor* subspecies have a single weak hinge between the abdominal and pectoral scutes of the plastron. *S. minor peltifer*, the stripe-necked musk turtle, differs from the loggerhead musk by the presence of strong stripes on its neck. The most widely known musk turtle, *S. odoratus*, the common musk turtle, or stinkpot as it is occasionally called, has a small plastron and two distinctive stripes on each side of the face that run back from the snout and go to either side of the eyes.

Five species of *Kinosternon* are found in the US. Probably the most easily recognized is the striped mud turtle, *K. baurii*. This turtle is small, even for mud turtles, and has three light stripes running the length of the carapace. As with all mud turtles, it has two strong plastral hinges. Overlapping geographically with the striped mud turtle is the common mud turtle, *K. subrubrum*. This turtle is also small but lacks the carapacial striping. It is rather nondescript, with only occasional markings on some animals. The markings are usually in the form of yellow

Table 4. The Mud and Musk Turtles

Latin Name	Common Name
Claudius angustatus	Narrow-bridge Musk
Staurotypus salvinii	Pacific Coast Giant Musk
Staurotypus triporcatus	Mexican Giant Musk
Kinosternon acutum	Tabasco Mud
Kinosternon alamosae	Alamos Mud
Kinosternon angustipons	Narrow-bridged Mud
Kinosternon baurii	Striped Mud
Kinosternon creaseri	Creaser's Mud
Kinosternon dunni	Dunn's Mud
Kinosternon f. flavescens	Yellow Mud
arizonense	Arizona Mud
durangoense	Durango Mud
Kinosternon herrerai	Herrara's Mud
Kinosternon h. hirtipes	Mexican Rough-footed Mud
chapalaense	Lake Chapala Mud
magdalense	San Juanico Mud
megacephalum	Viesca Mud
murrayi	Mexican Plateau Mud
tarascense	Patzcuaro Mud
Kinosternon integrum	Mexican Mud
Kinosternon l. leucostomum	White-lipped Mud
postinguinale	Southern White-lipped Mud
Kinosternon oaxacae	Oaxaca Mud
Kinosternon s. scorpioides	Scorpion Mud
abaxillare	Central Chipas Mud
albogulare	White-throated Mud
carajasensis	Carajas Mud
cruentatum	Red-cheeked Mud
seriei	Argentine Mud
Kinosternon s. sonoriense	Sonora Mud
longifemorale	Sonoyta Mud
Kinosternon s. subrubrum	Common Mud
hippocrepis	Mississippi Mud
steindachneri	Florida Mud
Sternotherus carinatus	Razor-backed Musk
Sternotherus depressus	Flattened Musk
Sternotherus m. minor	Loggerhead Musk
peltifer	Striped-neck Musk
Sternotherus odoratus	Common Musk

mottling or faint stripes on the head, especially in *K. s. hippocrepis*. This subspecies is sometimes confused with *K. baurii*, which it greatly resembles except for the carapacial striping.

Further west, one encounters the yellow mud turtle, *K. flavescens*. The carapace is a drab olive or brown, while the skin is yellow, ranging to grey. Two other species just enter the US: *K. sonoriense* and *K. hirtipes*. The Sonoran mud turtle is a medium-sized mud turtle, somewhat elongated, with an olive-brown carapace and grey skin with darker mottlings. Only one subspecies of the Mexican mud turtle, *K. hirtipes murrayi*, enters the US down in Texas. This species has three carapacial keels, while the skin is dark with a fine reticulated pattern on the head.

The majority of mud turtles are located in Mexico and Central and South America. A number of these, including *K. herrerai*, *K.*

Table 5. Maximum Size and Natural Range of the Mud and Musk Turtle

Species	Max Size	Range
Claudius angustatus	16.5 cm	Veracruz, Mexico to Belize
Staurotypus salvinii	25 cm	Eastern Oaxaca Mexico to El Salvador (Pacific side)
Staurotypus triporcatus	37.9 cm	Veracruz Mexico to northwest Honduras (Atlantic side)
Sternotherus carinatus	16 cm	Eastern Texas to Mississippi
Sternotherus depressus	11.5 cm	Alabama
Sternotherus m. minor	13.5 cm	Central Georgia to central Florida
peltifer	-	Southwest Virginia to Mississippi and Alabama
Sternotherus odoratus	13.6 cm	Canada to Florida, west to Texas andWisconsin
Kinosternon acutum	12 cm	From southern Mexico to Belize (Atlantic side)
Kinosternon alamosae	13.5 cm	Western coast of Mexico
Kinosternon angustipons	12 cm	Nicaragua to Panama (Caribbean side)
Kinosternon baurii	12 cm	Virginia to Florida
Kinosternon creaseri	12.1 cm	Yucatan Peninsula
Kinosternon dunni	17.5 cm	Columbia (Pacific coast side)
Kinosternon f. flavescens	16.5 cm	From Nebraska south through Texas into Mexico
arizonense	-	Southern Arizona and Mexico
durangoense	-	Chihuahua, Coahuila, Durango (Mexico)
Kinosternon herrerai	17 cm	Gulf coast of Mexico
Kinosternon h. hirtipes	18.2 cm	Valley of Mexico
chapalaense	-	Jalisco and Michoacan, Mexico
magdalense	-	Magdalena Valley, Michoacan, Mexico
megacephalum	-	Southwestern Coahuila, Mexico
murrayi	-	Texas and Chihuahua south to Jalisco and Michoacan
tarascense	-	Lago de Patzcuaro basin of Michoacan
Kinosternon integrum	20.2 cm	Sonora south to Oaxaca, Mexico
Kinosternon l. leucostomum	17.4 cm	Mexico to Nicaragua
postinguinale	-	Nicaragua to Ecuador
Kinosternon oaxacae	17.5 cm	Oaxaca, Mexico
Kinosternon s. scorpioides	27 cm	Panama to northern Peru
abaxillare	-	Chiapas, Mexico
albogulare	-	Honduras to Panama
carajasensis	13 cm	Central Brazil
cruentatum	-	Mexico to Honduras
seriei	-	Northern Argentina and Bolivia
Kinosternon s. sonoriense	17.5 cm	California to Arizona, south to Sonora and Chihuahua
longifemorale	-	Rio Sonoyta basin of Arizona and Sonora
Kinosternon s. subrubrum	12.5 cm	Eastern US (New York to northern Florida)
hippocrepis	-	Texas to Mississippi
steindachneri	-	Peninsula of Florida

angustipons, K. dunni, and K. creaseri, have only been cursorily described, especially with regard to the details of their natural history.

Some of the more distinguished species of mud turtles are K. leucostomum, the white-lipped mud turtle, and K. scorpioides, the scorpion mud turtle. The white-lipped mud turtle has a dark carapace and a yellow plastron. Befitting its name, the edges of its jaws are cream colored, sometimes interrupted by dark smudges. The scorpion mud turtle group (there are six recognized subspecies) contains the red-cheeked mud turtle, K. s. cruentatum, one of the most colorful of the mud turtles. Individuals of this subspecies are moderately large, with the carapace bearing three keels. The carapace itself is yellowish and the plastron shades into an orange cast. Most strikingly, the sides of the turtle's head can be red or orange, giving the turtle its common name. It is occasionally available in the pet trade.

Natural History Mud and musk turtle habitats vary between and within each species' range, but, in general, they prefer slow-moving or still bodies of water. Preferred locations often have soft bottoms, either consisting of sand or mud, and support a large amount of aquatic vegetation. As most mud and musk turtles are omnivorous, this vegetation can serve as food or can hide the insects that are also part of the turtles' diet. Many mud turtles will nose around in the soft muck probing for food.

While mud turtles are often considered to be largely aquatic in habit and rarely found out of the water, under certain circumstances they will spend time on land. There are reports of mud and musk turtles climbing small trees with branches that overhang the water and ending up many feet up in the air. Some mud turtles will estivate underground during the hottest part of the summer, especially if the local ponds dry up. When on land, they will often favor small shallow burrows dug into the soil. Female mud turtles will also be found on land when they are searching for a suitable area for nesting.

Although they are hardy and interesting pets, mud and musk turtles (loggerhead musk shown here) can be nippy turtles.

Hatchlings of some of the smaller mud and musk turtle species are among the smallest in the world. For example, hatchling *S. odoratus* are under an inch (approximately 20 mm) in length, while hatchling *K. baurii* can be as small as two-thirds of an inch (16.5 mm). Although mud and musk turtle hatchlings resemble their adult counterparts, some differences are noticeable. In particular, some species have more dramatic markings as hatchlings. The loggerhead musk turtle (*S. m. minor*) has a pinkish plastron, while the other subspecies, *S. m. peltifer*, has a yellow-orange cast to the plastron and a striped neck. It is possible that these colorations may be warning signs to predatory fish. In experiments with largemouth bass, fish initially attempted to eat hatchling turtles, but quickly learned to reject them. Apparently, the violent motions of the ingested hatchlings were harmful to the gills or digestive tract of the fish.

Interesting Facts In recent years, there has been a large amount of scientific debate over the degree of separation between *Sternotherus* and *Kinosternon*. Some researchers believe that the two genera should be combined into one genus (*Kinosternon*). Others favor maintaining the split. The controversy began in 1986 when scientists compared thirteen types of protein in eighteen species within the family Kinosternidae. The variation among the proteins was not great, and analysis of the data supported many of the conclusions of other researchers based on morphology. However, two members of *Kinosternon*, *K. baurii* and *K. subrubrum*, appeared to be more similar to members of *Sternotherus* than to other species of *Kinosternon* located in Central and South America. Based on this, *Sternotherus* was replaced with *Kinosternon* (i.e., *Sternotherus odoratus* becomes *Kinosternon odoratum*, etc.).

Mississippi mud turtles and other members of the family tend to walk along the bottom of streams and ponds rather than swim.

Some researchers have accepted this alteration, while others have continued to use both *Sternotherus* and *Kinosternon*. A few have even gone back and forth. I have opted to use both *Sternotherus* and *Kinosternon* in this book, but keep in mind that other books may only use *Kinosternon*. The information about the turtles is still valid; while their names may change, the turtles are still the same. To paraphrase the old saying, "A musk turtle by any Latin name would smell as sweet."

Suitability As Pets The mud and musk turtles that occur within the US are all excellent choices for captive maintenance or breeding programs. They are hardy, long-lived turtles, with relatively straightforward environmental and dietary requirements. A particularly important characteristic is their adult size; these turtles are among the smallest aquatic turtles. Their small size means that they can be accommodated indoors in turtle tanks that are smaller than would be required for the sliders or related turtles. While most mud and musk turtles are not as attractively colored as the sliders, maps, or painted turtles, their interesting behaviors, inquisitive personalities, and small size more than make up for that shortcoming. These turtles have my strongest recommendation, especially for novice turtle keepers.

Is It A Mud Or A Musk

To the untrained eye, many of the mud and musk turtle species appear very similar. Without a positive identification, obtaining information on a specific turtle can be almost impossible. Fortunately, two keys have been published that are of enormous utility in distinguishing the species of Kinosternon (and Sternotherus, although both keys place Sternotherus in Kinosternon). The first key is in Ernst and Barbour's *Turtles of the World* (page 73). The second key is in John Iverson's A Revised *Checklist with Distribution Maps of Turtles of the World* (pages 214-215).

Map Turtles
Species, Descriptions, and Range One of the most distinguished of turtles occurs almost entirely within the borders of the continental US. Turtles of the genus *Graptemys*, more commonly known as map turtles, range through a wide variety of habitats from Florida to Texas, and north to the Dakotas and Quebec, Canada. Although they superficially resemble sliders and painted turtles, map turtles have a number of unique features that set them apart from other semi-aquatic turtles found in the same area. They are a diverse group of turtles, with many beautifully marked species, each type possessing distinctive habits, diets, and environmental preferences.

Map turtles follow the general body plan of the more common sliders and painted turtles. However, unlike those turtles, most map turtles have a well-defined keel running down the middle of the carapace. In a number of species, this keel also has rather large knobs or spines jutting upward or backward. This feature is responsible for the map turtles' other common name: sawback turtles. The marginal scutes at the rear of the carapace also project backward in most map turtles, giving the back of the turtle a decidedly serrated appearance.

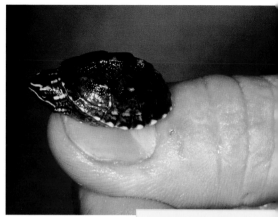

Hatchling common musk turtles are among the smallest turtles in the world.

Some species have a very large head and jaws designed to allow the turtle to crush snails and other mollusks. And finally, of course, the most noticeable difference is the reason that map turtles are so named: the distinctive thin lines covering the skin and scutes of the turtle, making it appear as if it were a contour or road map. These fine reticulations lend an air of beauty and elegance to the map turtle that is hard to equal.

Different species of map turtle are distinguished by the unique patterns of lines on the head and on the scutes. Another distinction is the size and shape of the spines or knobs on the carapacial keel. For example, *Graptemys nigrinoda*, the aptly named black-knobbed map turtle, has very characteristic large black knobs projecting straight up from the keel. *Graptemys oculifera*, the ringed map turtle, has a large orange or yellow ring on each scute on its carapace, while *Graptemys flavimaculata*, the yellow-blotched map turtle, has a solid yellow or orange blotch on its scutes.

Currently, there are approximately a dozen species of map turtle recognized, but this number varies depending on the authority being consulted. Some scientists consider certain species to be subspecies, rather than distinct species of their own. Also, it seems quite possible that there are other, still unrecognized species of map turtle inhabiting some remote sections of rivers in the central part of the country.

Natural History Habitats for map turtles vary depending on the species. Many seem to prefer rivers to ponds and lakes; in fact, some species are restricted to a single river drainage system. Species such as the common map, Ouachita map, and false map inhabit ponds and river-bottom swamps in addition to slow moving rivers. Other species (Texas map, black-knobbed map turtle, yellow-blotched map, and ringed) populate moderate to rapidly flowing streams with sandy or clay bottoms, although limestone-, mud-, and gravel-bottomed bodies of water also contain map turtles. No matter what type of habitat, abundant basking areas are essential.

In their natural habitat, most species of *Graptemys* are omnivorous eaters. However, the percentage of various types of food making up the turtles' diet varies from species to species, and, even in some cases, from males to females within a species. The species that develop broad jaws feed on mollusks and snails to a large extent, and, in females (whose head and jaws are even larger), this dietary preference can be even more pronounced. Other food items taken include insects, crawfish, worms, aquatic vegetation, and sometimes fish and carrion. In captivity, they have been known to eat fish, shellfish, chicken, liver, some types of lettuce, and insects, among things, although some species continue to require a diet composed mainly of snails, other mollusks, and crustaceans.

Map turtles are perhaps the shyest of our native aquatic turtles. Although they are avid baskers by nature, they are also extremely aware of their surroundings and will quickly enter the water at the slightest hint of danger. This wariness makes them much harder to observe than painted turtles or sliders. They prefer to use fallen trees and logjams as basking platforms, especially those that are surrounded by water. Because of their wary nature, many details of map turtle behavior in their natural environment have not yet been fully explored.

Among map turtles for which courtship and breeding behaviors have been described, some common behaviors have been noted.

Because they are nervous and sensitive to water quality, map turtles are best for experienced keepers. A common map is shown here.

Those species in which the males possess elongated claws apparently use them in approximately the same way as male sliders do. First, the male swims past the female and turns to face her. He then vibrates his forelimbs and elongated claws against her cheeks. After performing this courtship maneuver for a variable amount of time, the male will mount the female. In species in which the males lack long foreclaws, other behaviors have replaced this sequence. For example, it has been reported that the male Alabama map turtle will vibrate his head against the female's nose, alternating sides rapidly.

Female map turtles routinely lay multiple clutches during the course of a single breeding season. A moderate number of eggs are laid per clutch, ranging from 5 to 16 eggs, depending on the species. These hatch in 60 to 75 days. Females usually choose well-drained areas for egg deposition, such as sandy beaches or open clearings. The temperature at which the eggs incubate can affect the final sex of the turtle in some species of map turtle. Incubation at 25°C (77°F) gives a high percentage of male turtles, while eggs kept at 30°-35°C (86°-95°F) yield females, at least in *G. pseudogeographica*, *G. geographica*, and *G. ouachitensis*.

Interesting Facts Male turtles of some species (*G. flavimaculata*, *G. nigrinoda*, *G. oculifera*, *G. ouachitensis*, and *G. pseudogeographica*) possess elongated claws on their forefeet. Final adult size can be a distinguishing characteristic, as the sexes are quite different in adulthood. For many adults, the smallest female will be as large as or larger than the largest male. Finally, females of some species, most notably *G. barbouri*, *G. pulchra*, and *G. geographica*, develop very large, broad heads with heavy jaws, possibly to assist in eating hard-shelled mollusks.

Suitability As Pets Map turtles are not as common in captivity as sliders and painted turtles and when they are kept, it often seems that only a single individual, usually a male, is present (probably due to the smaller size of males). Map turtles can do well in captivity, but care must be taken to provide the proper type of arrangements. In most ways, their care is similar to that required for maintaining sliders and painted turtles.

Map turtles seem to be less tolerant of poor water conditions than other aquatic turtles. Water cleanliness and quality must be maintained for their health. If the water quality is not maintained, and the turtles do not have exposure to natural sunlight or a full-spectrum light source, they will develop mild fungal infections along the surface of their shells. Also, as map turtles are more nervous than other turtles, the location of their enclosure should also be chosen with care. Turtles in a high-traffic area may become stressed by the constant attention.

Table 6. Map Turtle Species and Natural Range

Scientific Name	Common Name	Range
Graptemys barbouri	Barbour's Map	Apalachicola and Chipola River drainage from Alabama to Florida
Graptemys caglei	Cagle's Map	Guadalupe and San Antonio River drainage in Texas
Graptemys ernsti	Ernst's Map	Pensacola Bay area of Florida and Alabama
Graptemys flavimaculata	Yellow-blotched Map	Pascagoula River drainage of Mississippi
Graptemys geographica	Common Map	Quebec and Vermont to Wisconsin, south to Kansas and Alabama
Graptemys gibbonsi	Gibbon's Map	Pascagoula and Pearl Rivers in Lousiana and Mississippi
Graptemys n. nigrinoda	Northern Black-knobbed Map	Tombigbee, Black Warrior & Alabama Rivers in Alabama & Mississippi
delticola	Southern Black-knobbed Map	
Graptemys oculifera	Ringed Map	Pearl River drainage in Louisiana and Mississippi
Graptemys o. ouachitensis	Ouachita Map	Minnesota to West Virginia, south to Louisiana and Oklahoma
sabinensis	Sabine Map	
Graptemys p. pseudogeographica	False Map	North Dakota to Ohio, south to Louisiana and Texas
kohnii	Mississippi Map	
Graptemys pulchra	Alabama Map	Eastern Louisiana to Western Florida
Graptemys versa	Texas Map	Colorado River drainage in Texas

This can also lead to shell injuries; turtles that are continually diving off their basking area in a panic are more likely to sustain compression injuries to the edges of their shells, leading to infections and possibly death. Map turtles' nervous dispositions should be taken into account, therefore, when initially setting up an enclosure, whether it be inside or outside.

Spotted turtles
Species, Descriptions, and Range Spotted turtles (*Clemmys guttata*) are small, aquatic turtles that are found along the east coast and the eastern Great Lakes region. They are very attractive turtles, with a smooth black shell, decorated with a variable number of bright yellow spots. The shell is longer than it is wide, and the species reaches an adult size of about 5 inches (12.7 cm). The spotted turtle's skin is also black with yellow spots. Males and females can be distinguished readily. Females have a yellow chin, orange eyes, and a flat

The yellow-blotched map turtle is one of the maps that has large black knobs on its carapace. .

plastron, while the males have a tan chin, brown eyes, a concave plastron, and a longer, thicker tail. The differences in coloration are apparent very early in life and can be used to sex hatchling turtles.

Three other *Clemmys* species are found in North America. All are relatively rare turtles, all of whose populations are endangered and protected in the states in which they occur. The wood turtle (*Clemmys insculpta*) is a much larger turtle that resembles the spotted turtle in shape, but does not have the black and yellow patterning. It is less aquatic than the spotted turtle. The bog turtle (*Clemmys muhlenbergii*) is smaller than the spotted turtle and only found in a few locations on the east coast. The western pond turtle (*Clemmys marmorata*) is found along the west coast from southern California north to Washington. Because of their protected status, none of these turtles are suitable for captive maintenance.

Natural History Spotted turtles are found in shallow water bodies, rather than deep rivers or lakes. They prefer slow-moving streams, ponds, and wetlands that have a muddy or sandy bottom, with abundant natural vegetation. They are active during the day, with a period of basking followed by a period of foraging, and the length of each period dependent on the ambient temperature. They are omnivorous, eating aquatic grasses and algae, insects and their larvae, snails, tadpoles, and crustaceans, plus any dead animals, birds, or fish that they might encounter.

Interesting Facts The spots on a spotted turtle's shell are actually transparent areas in the black pigmentation of the scutes. These clear areas allow the underlying yellow coloration to be seen. As these turtles age, they often darken in color, and some older adults lack spots because of this.

Suitability for Captive Maintenance Spotted turtles are easily maintained in captivity. Their small size, beautiful coloration, and interesting behavior and personality make them a desired species of turtle for many keepers. However, they are protected by law in their natural range because native populations are all threatened. These laws make it difficult to keep spotted turtles in captivity in many eastern states. If you wish to keep them, be sure to check into the legal status of the turtle in your state. Also, because of the pressure that wild populations are under, no wild-caught spotted turtle should be purchased. Spotted turtles are relatively easy to breed in captivity, and a turtle keeper interested in this species should seek out a breeder and purchase authentic captive-hatched turtles.

Other North American Species
Softshell Turtles
Species, Descriptions, and Range Softshell turtles are found throughout the world; in the US there are five different species, all belonging to the genus *Trionyx* (or *Apalone*, depending on which classification scheme is consulted). Two of these, *Trionyx sinensis* and *T. steindachneri*, are native to China, but have been introduced in Hawaii. The Florida softshell turtle (*Trionyx ferox*) is found mainly in Florida, although some populations are found in neighboring states. The smooth softshell (*Trionyx muticus*) is found in the central portion of the country, along the Mississippi, its tributaries, and some river basins to the west. The spiny softshell (*Trionyx spiniferus*) is found in the same region as the smooth softshell, but its range extends much farther to the east, north, and west, and there are isolated populations in a number of states, including Montana, California, New Mexico, Arizona, New York, and New Jersey.

All of the softshells found on the continental US are flat, oval turtles, with a rough leathery skin in place of the hard scutes found on other turtles. Their skin is usually a drab green or gray, usually with a pattern of dots and lines. Some species have a spot or ring patterning on their carapace. Their limbs are modified, resembling flippers. Their faces are long and pointed, ending in a slight flare

Note the tan chin and brown eyes of this spotted turtle. They indicate it is a male.

that houses two large nostrils. All of these turtles grow to a large size, with the females usually growing up to twice as big as the males. Florida softshell females can reach almost two feet (0.6 m) in length and spiny softshell females over 18 inches (45.7 cm), while smooth softshell females top out at over a foot (over 30.5 cm) in length.

Natural History Softshell turtles are almost exclusively aquatic. They live in rivers and permanent ponds or lakes that can be reached from those rivers. They are active during the day, foraging for their food, basking by floating on the surface (rather than on fallen trees or logs) or buried in mud or sand. They are mainly carnivorous, eating insects, snails, fish, and crayfish, although some turtles will consume certain types of plants. They are very aggressive turtles and are capable of inflicting very deep bites.

Suitability As Pets Softshell turtles are recommended only for the most dedicated and fastidious turtle keepers and are not suitable for beginners. They require very careful attention in order to do well in captivity. Their water needs to be very clean, as many of these turtles develop skin lesions if kept under less than pristine water conditions. For those enthusiasts that decide to keep softshell turtles, cage decorations should be kept to a minimum and sharp or rough objects should be avoided. The bottom should be lined with a few inches of very fine sand, in which the turtle will usually bury itself. The water level should allow the turtle to reach the surface with its long neck while still buried in the sand.

A basking area should be provided, but may not be used often. Beware of their deceptively long necks, as these turtles are very aggressive, prone to biting, and have a very long reach.

Getting Darker

The shells of adult turtles of many species become darker with age, losing their patterning or lighter coloration. Such individuals are usually referred to as melanistic turtles. The overall percentage of melanistic turtles varies from population to population, even within the same species.

Snapping Turtles
Species, Descriptions, and Range
Two different types of turtle are called snapping turtles: the common snapper (*Chelydra serpentina*) and the alligator snapper (*Macroclemys temmincki*). Both types are very large turtles—the common snapper reaches a carapace length of 18-20 inches ((45.7-50.8 cm), while the alligator snapper can reach lengths of 30 inches (76.2 cm). In addition to

Aquatic Turtles

Wood turtles are one of the least aquatic of the aquatic turtles. It is a protected species.

their size, they are very bulky turtles and appear much more massive than other similarly sized turtles. Adult alligator snappers can weigh upwards of 175 pounds (79.4 kg), for example. For this reason, they make very impressive display turtles, if their size can be accommodated.

There are four subspecies of the common snapper, ranging eastward from the Rocky Mountains and southward from Canada and as far south as Central America. The carapace is very heavy, but relatively smooth, while the plastron is greatly reduced in size, looking like a small cross. The head of the common snapper is massive, as are the limbs and tail. The tail is very heavy and long and has spines that project upward running down its length.

Only one species of alligator snapper is recognized; it occurs in the southern portion of the country, centered around the Mississippi River basin and its lower tributaries. The carapace is quite rough, with each scute taking on a roughly pyramidal shape. An alligator snapper's head is massive, but its limbs and tail are not quite as heavy-looking as those of the common snapper, and it has very low tail spines.

Natural History The common snapper is found in many different habitats, ranging from shallow streams to very deep lakes. It is usually found walking along the bottom, but can swim if required to do so. It will consume just about any food item that it can fit in its mouth or rip apart prior to eating. Snappers are solitary animals and rarely tolerate the presence of other snappers. Matings between snapping turtles are violent affairs that can leave both parties with injuries.

Alligator snappers are usually found in larger rivers but will enter ponds or marshes. They can tolerate the brackish water found at the mouths of rivers along the Gulf Coast. These snappers are omnivorous scavengers and ambush hunters. Their most famous attribute is a small pink lure located on their tongue that looks remarkably like a worm. An alligator snapper will rest on the river bottom with its mouth wide open and wriggle the lure until a fish enters its mouth in an attempt to bite the lure.

Both types of snapper are very aggressive animals, especially if encountered out of the water. Their large size and powerful jaws make them a threat to anyone who is not extremely careful around them.

Suitability As Pets Both species of snapping turtle are not suitable for most turtle keepers, although they are often available as captive-hatched juveniles from turtle farms in the US. While interesting in appearance as babies, they grow very rapidly, and the adult turtles reach unmanageable sizes quickly. Both species have a nasty disposition and are capable of inflicting severe bites on unwary keepers. In spite of all these drawbacks, some people do keep snappers—usually, as display animals or for educational purposes as part of a reptile show, for example. If their size and disposition can be accommodated, they are relatively easy to keep in captivity.

Exotic species
Reeves' Turtle
Species, Descriptions, and Range Pond turtles in the Middle East and Asia have been imported into the US in waves, and some have become established in breeding groups. These turtles occupy the same ecological niches in their native habitats that the sliders, cooters, and painted occupy in the US. One of the most commonly seen is the Reeves' turtle, *Chinemys reevesi*. However, unlike our native aquatic turtles, the Reeves' turtle is not saucer-shaped, but more rectangular overall. It is one of the smaller turtles available; most

Albino Florida softshells are bred in small numbers and cost much more than the normally colored ones.

Aquatic Turtles

animals only grow to about 5 inches (12.7 cm) in length. The shell of the Reeves' has three keels, or ridges, running the length of the carapace from head to tail.

Coloration of the Reeves' turtle varies widely from individual to individual. The shell can range from a yellowish brown to a dark brown or black shade, while the skin can range from an olive or grey-green shade to black. In the lighter animals, there are series of white or yellow lines running along the sides of the neck and head. The black animals tend to lack this striping.

There are only a couple of features that vary between male and female Reeves' turtles. The first sexual dimorphism is the size and shape of the tail. The male has a longer tail, with a pronounced bulge at its base. As in many male turtles, the vent opening on the tail is beyond the edge of the carapace. The second difference is the presence of a slight concavity in the plastron of the male turtle. This is not very deep, however, and is not as good an indicator as the tail differences. In addition to these differences, it is possible that the darker, nearly black, turtles are more likely to be male, while the brown and olive green animals are more likely to be female, as the males tend to become more melanistic with age. Certainly, among the numerous Reeves' turtles I have examined, most, if not all, of the black individuals were male turtles. This dimorphism may not be present in all populations, or there may be different subspecies involved.

The Reeves' turtle comes from mainland China and Japan, where it is found in great abundance in a number of areas. It is also found in Korea, Taiwan, and Hong Kong. It usually lives in ponds, streams, and canals that are relatively shallow and have muddy or sandy bottoms. Turtles will frequently leave the water to bask on rocks or logs. The Reeves' is not a nocturnal turtle and can be seen foraging for food during the day, much like the sliders and painted turtles common to much of the US. Two other species of *Chinemys* exist: *Chinemys kwangtungensis* and *Chinemys megalocephala*. Both species are relatively rare, although *Chinemys kwangtungensis* is occasionally available from dealers.

The alligator snapper wriggles the pink appendage on its tongue to lure fish into its mouth.

Natural History The Reeves' turtle is an omnivore. In the wild, it eats insects, frogs, fish, and aquatic plants. In captivity, it will take raw liver, steak, beef heart, cooked chicken, lettuce, pear, cantaloupe, earthworms, mealworms, crickets, monkey chow, and the commercial turtle foods. This turtle is quite a voracious eater and will overeat if provided with sufficient food.

The Reeves' turtle has a wide variety of behaviors, making it a fascinating animal to observe. These turtles are somewhat cold hardy and will remain active at lower than normal temperatures, but this is not an optimal situation for them. I maintain my turtles at approximately 70° to 72°F (about 21°-22°C), slightly higher than room temperature. Females will usually lay two or three eggs at a time. These can be incubated at a temperature of 78° to 85°F (about 26-29°C). Hatching should occur in about 80 days.

The greatest problem with the Reeves' turtle is the condition of newly imported animals. Often, they have an infection that causes the scutes of the shell to peel up and separate from the underlying tissue. Although not immediately life-threatening, it takes quite a bit of time and effort to eliminate the infection and does detract from the appearance of the animal. The large number of animals with this problem is probably due to the conditions that they are kept under during importation or during the distribution process to pet shops. Luckily, the success in captive breeding this turtle has reduced this problem, as captive-bred animals are usually free of these types of infections and are usually not shipped and held in mass quantities.

One of the more available Asian pond turtles—and one of the hardiest—is Reeves' turtle.

Suitability As Pets These turtles are one of the best choices for an exotic turtle pet because of their hardy nature, interesting personality, and moderate size—provided you start with a captive-hatched animal to avoid the possibility of shell infections. In captivity, the Reeves' turtle can be kept in the same way that one would keep an ordinary slider or painted turtle. It does quite well in an outdoor pen in that has a pool for swimming or in an indoor aquarium. If kept indoors, an individual adult turtle does well in a 30-gallon (113.6 l) aquarium, while a pair should be housed in at least a 40-gallon (151.4 l) aquarium. The Reeves' turtle is quite active and so minimal decoration of the tank is suggested, as they may quickly destroy any plantings. However, be sure to position flat smooth rocks or wood above water under a lamp to provide areas for the turtle to leave the water, dry off, and bask.

African Mud Turtles (*Pelusios* Species)

Species, Descriptions, and Range Turtles in the genus *Pelusios* grow to a moderate size, with the largest (*P. sinuatus*) reaching a length of approximately 18 inches (45.7 cm). The smallest (*P. nanus*) only reaches a size of 4.5 inches (11.4 cm). A strong hinge on the plastron is a distinguishing feature of the genus *Pelusios*.

African mud turtles have carapaces that range in shape from oval to almost round; the carapace itself is not strongly domed. Generally, they resemble the sliders and painted turtles of North America. Most species of *Pelusios* are not strongly colored; the carapace usually is some shade of brown or black, while the plastron ranges from yellow to black. The skin color ranges from gray through brown to yellow. While most species are relatively undistinguished, some do possess some attractive patterning. Some animals have distinctive dark and light patterns on the plastron; these can be useful in distinguishing between species. *P. b. bechuanicus* has a contrasting pattern of yellow stripes on its face, while the faces of a number of species have a fine yellow vermiculation on a dark background. Many species have two or three short barbels on the chin and a bright ring around the iris of the eye.

Natural History In their natural environment, African mud turtle species are carnivorous or omnivorous. In captivity, they have been reported to take many of the foods normally fed to North

Other Asian Pond Turtles

A number of other turtle species that superficially resemble the Reeves' turtle are occasionally imported from Asia and the Middle East. These include the Asian pond and leaf turtles (*Mauremys* and *Cyclemys* species) and the stripe-necked turtles (*Ocadia*). Many of these turtles are also suitable for captive maintenance, but take care to identify the turtle correctly so that you can provide the appropriate environmental conditions and meet its dietary requirements.

American turtles, including various vegetables, fish, earthworms, insects, and prepared foods such as turtle or trout chows. However, the proportion of vegetable to animal matter preferred will vary between species.

Pelusios species can be maintained at temperatures that are suitable for sliders and painted turtles: from the mid-70's to the mid-80's (about 23°-30°C). Captive African mud turtles have been known to estivate in underground burrows when the temperature gets too warm. When conditions return to a suitable level, the estivating turtles reemerge and become active once again.

Specialist breeders produce small numbers of *Chinemys kwangtungensis* for sale. This is a hatchling.

Although maintenance of *Pelusios* presents little difficulty, breeding is a different matter. Although African mud turtles have been bred in captivity, much of this breeding has occurred in zoos and other institutions that acquired a documented population of a specific species. In contrast, many of the turtles entering the country for the pet trade will be sold as individuals with little accompanying documentation. Also, differences between species of *Pelusios* can be relatively subtle. The combination of these two problems means that it may be quite difficult to locate a suitable mate for an individual African mud turtle.

Suitability As Pets African mud turtles have been reaching North American markets in increasing numbers in the past few years. As they are relatively hardy, of moderate size, and fairly abundant in their natural range, they have been collected in large numbers, and so enter the pet trade as a cheap exotic turtle. Their natural ability to survive periods of deprivation probably contributes to their increasing exploitation. Fortunately, because of this hardiness, most turtles generally arrive in reasonably good condition. Most of the species of *Pelusios* are relatively undemanding in their needs, so they usually prosper under conditions suitable for North American turtles such as sliders and painted turtles. As more turtle breeders work with this group, captive-born hatchlings should become available in greater numbers. This is fortunate because African side-neck turtles are a good choice for captive maintenance.

South American and Australian Snake-Necked Turtles

Species, Descriptions, and Range Snake-necked turtles are very distinctive and unique looking animals, with very long necks coming from a normal looking turtle shell. Surprisingly, the long neck of the snake-necked turtle has developed separately on opposite sides of the world—in South America and in Australia. Both are pleurodiran turtles, but those of the genus *Chelodina* are found in Australia and New Guinea, while the turtles in the genus *Hydromedusa* are located in South America. The Australia/New Guinea group is more numerous; approximately a dozen different species have been identified. They are all medium to large turtles, with the maximum carapace size ranging from 9-18 inches (22.8-45.7 cm). The necks on these turtles can extend from 60 to 75 percent of the carapace length.

The South American snake-necked turtles consist of two species within *Hydromedusa*: *Hydromedusa tectifera* and *Hydromedusa maximiliani*. Both occur in Brazil, but *H. tectifera* is also found in Paraguay, Uruguay, and Argentina. These South American snake-necks do not grow as large as the Australian forms, only reaching a carapacial length of 8-12 inches (20.3-30.5 cm). However, their necks are relatively longer—approximately the same length as their carapace.

Natural History Most of the *Chelodina* turtles are carnivorous or omnivorous. They inhabit a wide variety of bodies of water, from slow-moving rivers to lakes to temporary ponds. Many species have been shown to estivate in the dried mud when the water evaporates during the hottest times of the year.

The *Hydromedusa* species inhabit slow-moving rivers, lakes, and ponds. They are carnivorous, but very little is known about their habits in their native environment. They are not as aggressive as the Australian snake-necked turtles.

Pelusios subniger is the most frequently available of the African mud turtles. It is sometimes sold as the East African black mud turtle.

Totally Different, Yet Almost Identical

African mud turtles differ from all of the North American turtles in a fundamental way—the manner in which they retract their heads into their shells. North American turtles, such as the Red-eared slider, are all cryptodiran (hidden-necked) turtles, while African mud turtles are pleurodiran (side-necked). However, even though they exhibit this fundamental difference, the lifestyle and habitat of the African mud turtle and the Red-eared slider are very similar, and so these two turtle groups require similar care in captivity.

Suitability As Pets The Australian and New Guinea snake-necked turtles make relatively hardy and interesting display animals, if specimens can be found. They are not particularly common in captivity, but captive breeding has been successful, and more of them are starting to become available. Wild-caught turtles are rare, as Australia does not export any of its wildlife. Captive maintenance of these turtles is similar to that required for the southern forms of the North American sliders.

The South American snake-necked turtles are not common in captivity. From the few reports on their captive maintenance, they appear to be a rather delicate type of turtle and are prone to shell infections. Wild-caught individuals do not adapt readily to commercial turtle food, preferring live fish and other prey. The captive maintenance of these turtles should only be attempted by experienced turtle keepers.

The Matamata

Species, Descriptions, and Range Among the small number of truly unique turtles, the matamata has a distinguished place of honor. Anyone who has ever seen a matamata will instantly recognize it again. The Latin name for this side-necked turtle, *Chelus fimbriatus*, means "fringed turtle," a description which, although accurate, hardly does it justice. A matamata's most striking features are its head and neck region. Viewed from above, the head is a broad triangle in shape, with a very long, slender snout forming one tip of the triangle. All along the head and long, muscular neck are small, multi-branched tufts or flaps of flesh that give the turtle its Latin name. These loose tufts drift and sway with any current in the water or movement of the turtle, making the turtle appear as if it was covered with weeds or algae.

The matamata grows to be fairly large; turtles with a carapace length of 16-18 inches (40.6-45.7 cm) have been captured. In adults, the carapace is usually black or brown with some orange color, while the plastron ranges in color from a light yellow to a deeper brown shade. The hatchlings are bright pink to orange. Each individual scute can be fairly rough in appearance, due to the way that the scute grows. Three keels run the length of the carapace; these keels result from the center of each scute raising up to form a knob, with the highest knobs at the back of the carapace. The skin of the matamata varies from an orange-brown to a grey-brown tone.

Ambush Turtle

The matamata is one of the most instantly recognizable turtles in the world, but only to human eyes. Its bizarre head shape, fringed skin, and mottled coloration all serve to camouflage the turtle in its natural environment, making it virtually invisible to the fish it preys upon from ambush.

Natural History All of the physical features of the matamata aid it in its natural environment. Algae grows on the roughened carapace, causing it to look like an old, encrusted rock. The tufts and fringes along the neck and head may act as a type of camouflage, breaking up the turtle's outline to further disguise it. There is some debate as to whether or not the flaps of skin also serve as sensory mechanisms to allow the turtle to detect nearby movement.

The giant snake-necked turtle (*Chelodina expansa*) is Australia's largest freshwater turtle, reaching a carapace length of nearly 20 inches (50 cm.).

Finally, the color of its shell and skin allows the matamata to blend in to its surroundings.

The use of camouflage and disguise gives the matamata the chance to take full advantage of its environment in hunting for food. The matamata inhabits muddy, sometimes stagnant, shallow pools and streams in northern South America, where it ranges as far west as Ecuador and

Peru, as far south as Bolivia and central Brazil, and as far north as Colombia and Venezuela. Looking like a pile of rocks or debris, a hungry turtle rests quietly on the bottom, occasionally stretching its long neck up until its snorkel-like nose can be used to take a breath. It will remain almost motionless underwater until a fish comes too close to its mouth. At this point, the turtle thrusts out its head and opens its large mouth as wide as possible. This acts like a vacuum cleaner; the prey and a large amount of water are rapidly sucked into the turtle's mouth and throat, which can be stretched out quite a bit. The matamata snaps its mouth shut, the water is slowly expelled, and the fish is swallowed whole. The prey has to be appropriately sized for the turtle; matamatas cannot chew very well due to the way their mouths are constructed. Matamatas in the wild may use other methods in addition to the ambush approach to capture prey. Occasionally, some specimens in captivity have been observed slowly herding fish into a confined area before sucking them into their mouths.

The odd appearance of the matamata serves as camouflage as it waits on the bottom of streams for prey to pass by.

Suitability As Pets The matamata generally does reasonably well in captivity, provided that its modest requirements are met. The matamata requires a moderately large aquarium with a large surface area, but not much depth. Its sedentary lifestyle allows it to do well in an enclosure smaller than would be necessary for a more active turtle of its size, making it an even more coveted display animal. Perhaps due to their large size, awkwardness, or

Matamatas catch their prey by quickly opening their mouths and sucking in the hapless fish.

the nature of their normal environment, adult matamatas rarely swim, preferring instead to walk slowly along the bottom. Therefore, the water should be shallow enough that the turtle can stretch its neck up and breathe without moving off of the bottom of the tank, yet deep enough that the animal is fully submersed at all times.

The tank does not need to have excess items; matamatas don't bask, and so basking logs or rocks are not needed. A land section is also usually not required unless breeding is expected, in which case an area for egg deposition is a necessity. Water condition is important for the long-term health of this turtle. In addition to requiring clean, slow-moving water, the water should be slightly acidic, and peat moss is often added to aid in this.

The feeding of a captive matamata is relatively straightforward. Most animals require live prey of an appropriate size—the turtle must be able to swallow the fish whole. Bait fish such as minnows are the usual food offered to matamatas. Although goldfish could be used, some people have reported having problems when turtles are fed exclusively on goldfish. Food fish should probably be kept in a separate aquarium for a few days or longer prior to feeding to the turtle. This allows time to flush out any drugs or chemicals in the fish's system, allows time for it to be fed a high-protein, high-vitamin fish food, and allows time to observe the fish for signs of disease. Some turtles will adapt to eating chopped fish or other types of meat, which can be used to increase the variety of food offered to the turtle.

E very pet owner hopes that their pet will live a long and healthy life. Those who keep turtles are no exception, but turtle keepers face a problem that is not encountered with many other pets. With proper care and attention, turtles can be very long-lived, and so a turtle keeper may need to address the possibility that their pet may outlive them. A musk turtle (*Sternotherus odoratus*) was kept at the Philadelphia Zoo for 54 years. It did not die of old age but perished in an accident. It is quite likely that this turtle could have lived for decades more. Even teenagers who obtain a turtle as a pet may be faced with the possibility that they will still be caring for that turtle on their 70th birthday. This level of long-range planning is beyond many of us, but should be considered when you first think about keeping turtles.

Once you have a turtle in your care, you should determine a course of action that will be followed if you become incapacitated or die. As with other types of pets, a section of your will should include your wishes for your turtle. Arrangements can be made with fellow turtle keepers where you live, for example. Turtles are not as visible as dogs or cats and may be overlooked in the general confusion that usually attends serious illness or death. Keep in mind that most zoos will not be able to accept individual turtles from private individuals, so other options must be considered. Many herpetological societies have adoption programs and accept turtles for

Concluding Remarks

relocation to new homes. However, placement through an adoption program means that you will have no voice in where your turtles go. If it is important to you that you know how your turtles are going to be cared for, you should make arrangements in advance, and reconfirm these arrangements periodically. In conclusion, if you have set up a course of action that is to be followed in the event of accident, illness, or death, your animals will not be neglected and you can be assured that they will continue to prosper.

Turtles are fascinating animals. They can be kept successfully in captivity, and if their needs are provided for appropriately, they will live for decades. This book has provided you with the basic framework for achieving that goal, but because it is meant to be an overview of turtle-keeping, it cannot provide extensive detail regarding certain specialized aspects of turtle care, such as breeding or managing an exotic turtle species that requires very specialized environmental conditions. However, a number of books are available that can provide this information. If you are interested in learning more, I strongly urge you to purchase and read those books. The References lists a number of the more readily available and detailed books; they would serve as a very good place to begin your research. I also urge you to seek out your local herpetological society. You may be living within a few blocks of one of the best turtle keepers in the world and wouldn't otherwise know it! The herpetological and turtle societies listed in the Resources will serve as a starting point for you.

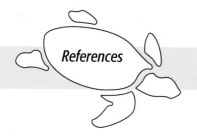

References

Turtle Care

Cobb, Jo. *Turtles and Terrapins: A Complete Introduction.* 1987. Neptune City, NJ: TFH Publications.

Gurley, Russ. *Keeping and Breeding Freshwater Turtles.* 2003. Rochester, MN: Living Art Publishing.

Highfield, Andy C. *A Practical Encyclopedia of Keeping and Breeding Tortoises and Freshwater Turtles.* 1996. London: Carapace Press.

Specific Turtles Species

Cann, John. *Australian Freshwater Turtles.* 1998. United Kingdom: Beaumont Publishing.

Ernst, Carl H., Lovich, Jeffrey E., and Roger W. Barbour. *Turtles of the United States and Canada.* 1994. Washington, DC: Smithsonian Institution Press.

Gibbons, J. Whitfield. *Life History and Ecology of the Slider Turtle.* 1990. Washington, DC: Smithsonian Institution Press.

Mara, W. P. *Map Turtles and Diamondback Terrapins.* 1996. Neptune City, NJ: TFH Publications.

Pritchard, Peter C. H., and Pedro Trebbau. *The Turtles of Venezuela.* 1984. Salt Lake City: Society for the Study of Amphibians and Reptiles.

Tikader, B. K., and R. C. Sharma. *Handbook Indian Testudines.* 1985. Calcutta: Zoological Survey of India.

Walls, Jerry G. *Cooters, Sliders and Painted Turtles.* 1996. Neptune City, NJ: TFH Publications.

General Reference

Ernst, Carl H., and Roger W. Barbour, *Turtles of the World.* 1989. Washington, DC: Smithsonian Institution Press.

Iverson, John B. *A Revised Checklist with Distribution Maps of the Turtles of the World.* 1992. Privately Printed.

Obst, Fritz J. *Turtles, Tortoises and Terrapins.* 1988. New York: St. Martin's Press.

Pritchard, Peter C. H. *Encyclopedia of Turtles.* 1979. Neptune City, NJ: TFH Publications.

Turtle Conservation Fund. *A Global Action Plan for Conservation of Tortoises and Freshwater Turtles: Strategy and Funding Prospectus 2002-2007.* 2002. Lunenburg, MA: Conservation International and Chelonian Research Foundation.

Van Dijk, Peter Paul, Stuart, Bryan L., and Anders G. J. Rhodin (Eds.). *Asian Turtle Trade: Proceedings of a Workshop on Conservation and Trade of Freshwater Turtles and Tortoises in Asia (Chelonian Research Monographs Number 2).* 2000. Lunenburg, MA: Chelonian Research Foundation.

Author's Note: A number of these books are out of print. Local libraries may have copies available, especially in larger cities. Copies may also be available for reading at university libraries. Some herpetological societies maintain reading libraries for their members. Finally, online book dealers may be able to locate individual copies.

Photo Credits:

Marian Bacon: 36, 110, 118

Joan Balzarini: 72, 73

R. D. Bartlett: back cover, 1, 13, 29, 41, 48, 66, 70, 81, 87, 88, 94, 114

Jon Boxall: 83

Vince Brach: 8, 17, 100

Robbie Cohen: 42

Suzanne L. Collins: 22, 103, 106, 109

Isabelle Francais: 3, 85, 107

Paul Freed: 102

James E. Gerholdt: 32, 38, 43

David T. Kirkpatrick: 35, 47, 51, 53, 54, 78, 96

Barry Mansell: 92

W. P. Mara: 62, 71

Sean McKeown: 19, 112

Aaron Norman: front cover, 4, 16, 24, 30, 64, 68, 117, 120

Mella Panzella: 6, 21

Mark Smith: 79, 115, 119

K. H. Switak: 12, 33, 45, 55, 59, 60, 65, 76, 90, 99, 111

John Tyson: 57, 84

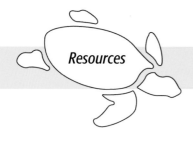

Clubs & Societies
United States

American Society of Ichthyologists and Herpetologists
Maureen Donnelly, Secretary
Grice Marine Laboratory
Florida International University
Biological Sciences
11200 SW 8th St.
Miami, FL 33199
Telephone: (305) 348-1235
E-mail: asih@fiu.edu
www.asih.org

California Turtle & Tortoise Society:
http://www.tortoise.org/index.html

Chicago Turtle Club
The Chicago Turtle Club
c/o Lisa Koester
6125 N. Fairfield Ave.
Chicago, IL 60659
chicagoturtle@geocities.com
http://www.geocities.com/Heartland/Village/7666/

Florida Turtle Conservation Trust
Florida Turtle Conservation Trust
c/o George L. Heinrich
1213 Alhambra Way S.
St. Petersburg, FL 33705-4620
http://www.ftct.org/

Gulf Coast Turtle and Tortoise Society
1227 Whitestone
Houston, Texas 77073
Information Line: 281-443-3383
info@gctts.org
http://www.gctts.org/

Mid-Atlantic Turtle & Tortoise Society
P.O. Box 23686
Baltimore, MD 21203
matts@matts-turtles.org
http://www.matts-turtles.org/

The National Turtle and Tortoise Society
P.O. Box 66935
Phoenix, AZ 85082-6935

NTTS info line: 602-ASK-NTTS (602-275-6887)
askntts@ntts-az.org
http://www.ntts-az.org/

New York Turtle and Tortoise Society
NYTTS
P.O. Box 878
Orange, NJ 07051-0878
QandA@nytts.org
http://nytts.org/

Rio Grande Turtle and Tortoise Club
Albuquerque NM
http://www.rgttc.org/
rgttc@yahoo.com

Sacramento Turtle and Tortoise Club
S.T.T.C. (Sacramento Turtle and Tortoise Club)
25 Starlit Circle
Sacramento, CA 95831
http://ourworld.compuserve.com/homepages/felicerood/

San Diego Turtle and Tortoise Society
P.O. Box 712514
Santee, CA 92072-2514
(619) 593-2123
Care.Consultant@sdturtle.org
http://www.sdturtle.org/

Seattle Turtle and Tortoise Club
23908 Bothell Everett Hwy
B-103
Bothell, WA 98021
http://www.geocities.com/seattleturtleclub/

Society for the Study of Amphibians and Reptiles (SSAR)
Marion Preest, Secretary
The Claremont Colleges
925 N. Mills Ave.
Claremont, CA 91711
Telephone: 909-607-8014
E-mail: mpreest@jsd.claremont.edu
www.ssarherps.org

Turtle and Tortoise Club of Florida
P.O. box 950516
Lake Mary, Florida 32795-0516
http://members.aol.com/scooterfl/

Turtle and Tortoise Preservation Group
836 2nd Street NW
Rochester, MN 55901
http://www.ttpg.org/

Turtle Survival Alliance
http://www.turtlesurvival.org/

International
British Chelonia Group
P.O.Box 1176
Chippenham Wilts
SN15 1XB
UK

German Chelonia Group
http://www.dght.de/ag/schildkroeten/english/eschildkroet
en.htm

Irish Association of Tortoise Keepers
http://homepage.eircom.net/~090316/index.html

Ontario Turtle & Tortoise Society
P.O. Box 52149
307 Robinson St.
Oakville, Ontario, Canada
L6J 7N5
http://members.aol.com/WALDIAL/otts.htm

The Tortoise Trust
Tortoise Trust
BM Tortoise
London
WC1N 3XX
UK
http://www.tortoisetrust.org/

World Chelonian Trust
PMB #292
685 Bridge St Plaza
Owatonna, MN 55060
http://www.chelonia.org/

Veterinary Resources

Association of Reptile and Amphibian Veterinarians
P.O. Box 605
Chester Heights, PA 19017
Phone: 610-358-9530
Fax: 610-892-4813
ARAVETS@aol.com
www.arav.org

Rescue And Adoption Services

American Tortoise Rescue
23852 Pacific Coast Highway #928

Malibu, CA 90265
www.tortoise.com

ASPCA
424 East 92nd Street
New York, NY 10128-6801
Phone: (212) 876-7700
information@aspca.org
www.aspca.org

Massachusetts Turtle Rescue
http://www.maturtlerescue.org/

RSPCA (UK)
Wilberforce Way
Southwater
Horsham, West Sussex RH13 9RS
Telephone: 0870 3335 999
www.rspca.org.uk

Turtle Homes (worldwide)
http://www.turtlehomes.org/

Turtle Survival Alliance
504 Ladin Lane
Lakeway TX 78734
Telephone: 512-608-9882
Lisa@TurtleCenter.org
http://www.turtlesurvival.org/

Websites

Turtle and Tortoise Club
http://www.tortoise.org/

Chelonian Research Foundation
http://www.chelonian.org/

Magazines

Tortoise Tracks (Online Magazine)
http://www.tortoise-tracks.org/tt.html

The Tortuga Gazette
P.O. Box 7300
Van Nuys, CA 91409-7300
http://www.tortoise.org/cttc/gazette.html

Herp Digest
www.herpdigest.org

Reptiles
P.O. Box 6050
Mission Viejo, CA 92690
www.animalnetwork.com/reptiles

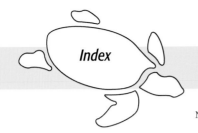

Index

Note: Boldface numbers indicate illustrations; an italic t indicates a table.